PORT...

THE EAST INDIA CO...
MOST POWERF...

TIRTHANKAR ROY teaches economic history at the London School of Economics and Political Science. His book *The Economic History of India 1857–1947*, now in its third edition, has changed the way Indian economic history is studied and taught worldwide.

GURCHARAN DAS is a world-renowned author, commentator and public intellectual. His bestselling books include *India Unbound* and *The Difficulty of Being Good*; his newest book is *India Grows at Night*. A graduate of Harvard University, Das was CEO of Procter & Gamble India before he took early retirement to become a full-time writer. He lives in Delhi.

THE STORY OF INDIAN BUSINESS

Arthashastra: The Science of Wealth by Thomas R. Trautmann

The World of the Tamil Merchant: Pioneers of International Trade by Kanakalatha Mukund

The Mouse Merchant: Money in Ancient India by Arshia Sattar

The East India Company: The World's Most Powerful Corporation by Tirthankar Roy

Caravans: Punjabi Khatri Merchants on the Silk Road by Scott C. Levi

Globalization before Its Time: Gujarati Traders in the Indian Ocean by Chhaya Goswami (edited by Jaithirth Rao)

Three Merchants of Bombay: Business Pioneers of the Nineteenth Century by Lakshmi Subramanian

The Marwaris: From Jagat Seth to the Birlas by Thomas A. Timberg

THE STORY OF INDIAN BUSINESS

THE EAST INDIA COMPANY

*The World's
Most Powerful Corporation*

TIRTHANKAR ROY

Introduction by
Gurcharan Das

PORTFOLIO
PENGUIN

PORTFOLIO

Published by the Penguin Group

Penguin Books India Pvt. Ltd, 7th Floor, Infinity Tower C, DLF Cyber City, Gurgaon 122 002, Haryana, India

Penguin Group (USA) Inc., 375 Hudson Street, New York, New York 10014, USA

Penguin Group (Canada), 90 Eglinton Avenue East, Suite 700, Toronto, Ontario, M4P 2Y3, Canada

Penguin Books Ltd, 80 Strand, London WC2R 0RL, England

Penguin Ireland, 25 St Stephen's Green, Dublin 2, Ireland (a division of Penguin Books Ltd)

Penguin Group (Australia), 707 Collins Street, Melbourne, Victoria 3008, Australia

Penguin Group (NZ), 67 Apollo Drive, Rosedale, Auckland 0632, New Zealand

Penguin Books (South Africa) (Pty) Ltd, Block D, Rosebank Office Park, 181 Jan Smuts Avenue, Parktown North, Johannesburg 2193, South Africa

Penguin Books Ltd, Registered Offices: 80 Strand, London WC2R 0RL, England

First published in Allen Lane by Penguin Books India 2012
Published in Portfolio 2016

ISBN 9780143426172

Typeset in Aldine401 BT by SÜRYA, New Delhi
Printed at Replika Press Pvt. Ltd, India

A PENGUIN RANDOM HOUSE COMPANY

CONTENTS

INTRODUCTION

THE EAST INDIA Company is a bridge which connects the pre-modern with the modern period in history, and Tirthankar Roy's book is a slim, elegant and authoritative guide for someone who wishes to make the crossing. His volume is part of a multi-volume history series by Penguin on the great business and economic ideas that have shaped commerce on the Indian subcontinent. Leading contemporary scholars will interpret these ideas in a lively, sharp and authoritative manner for the intelligent reader with no prior background in the field. Each slender volume recounts the romance and adventure of business enterprise in the bazaar or on the high seas along a 5000-mile coastline.

Based generally on a close examination of one or more classical texts, each author offers an enduring perspective on business and economic enterprise in the past, avoiding the pitfall of simplistically cataloguing a set of lessons for today. The value of the exercise, I believe, is to promote in the reader a longer term sensibility which can help one to understand the material bases for our present human condition and to think sensibly about the future. Taken together, the series as a whole celebrates the ideal captured in the Sanskrit word artha, 'material well being', which was one of the aims of the classical Indian life.

The books in this series range over a vast territory, beginning with a commentary on the two-thousand-year-old art of wealth, the *Arthashastra*, by the renowned Tom Trauttman, and ending with the *Bombay Plan*, drawn up by eminent industrialists in 1944–45, who wrestled with the proper roles of the public and private sectors, recounted for us vividly by Medha Kudaisiya. In between is a veritable feast. Four sparkling volumes cover the ancient and early medieval periods—Gregory Schopen presents the *Business Model of Early Buddhist Monasticism* based on the *Mulasarvastivada-vinaya*; Kanakalatha Mukund takes us into the world of the Tamil merchant drawn from the epics, *Silappadikaram* and *Manimekalai*, to the end of the Chola empire; Himanshu Prabha Ray transfers us to the maritime trading world of the western Indian ocean, along the Kanara and Gujarat coasts, using the Sanskrit

Lekhapaddhati written in Gujarati; and Arshia Sattar recounts the brilliant adventures of *The Mouse Merchant* and other tales based on *Kathasaritsagara* and other sources.

Scott Levi takes off into the early modern period with the saga of Multani traders in caravans through central Asia, rooted in the work of Zia al-Din Barani's *Tarikh-i Firuz Shahi* and Jean-Baptiste Tavernier. The celebrated Sanjay Subrahmanyam and Muzaffar Alam take us into the world of sultans, shopkeepers and portfolio capitalists in Mughal India. Ishan Chakrabarti traces the ethically individualistic world of Banarsidas, a Jain merchant in Mughal times, via his diary, *Ardhakathanak*. This present volume on the East India Company is, of course, our passage into the modern world. In another volume the distinguished Lakshmi Subramanian recounts the ups and downs in the adventurous lives of three great merchants of Bombay—Tarwady Arjunjee Nathjee, Jamsetjee Jeejeebhoy and Premchand Raychand.

Anuradha Kumar creates a narrative on the building of railways in nineteenth-century India through the eyes of those who built them. Chhaya Goswami dives deep into the Indian Ocean to recount the tale of Kachchhi enterprise in the triangle between Zanzibar, Muscat and Mandvi. Tom Timberg revisits the bold, risk-taking world of the Marwaris and Raman Mahadevan describes Nattukottai Chettiars' search for fortune. Vikramjit Banerjee rounds up the series with competing visions of prosperity among men who fought for India's freedom in the early twentieth century via the works of Gandhi, Vivekananda, Nehru, Ambedkar and others. The privilege of reading most of the rich and diverse volumes in this series has left me—one reader—with a sense of wonder at the vivid, dynamic and illustrious role played by trade and economic enterprise in advancing Indian civilization.

The modern corporation is a child of the East India Company

Since there is no point in going over the same territory as Tirthankar Roy's excellent book, I shall focus in this introduction on a few themes which highlight the enduring legacy of the East India Company (henceforth 'the Company'): the corporate model of doing business; the noble sentiment of trust and its relationship to contracts in the business life; the damaging effects of the Company's monopoly and its influence on Adam Smith's foundational text on capitalism; how the Company made its second fortune in China through opium; and, finally, what is the enduring significance of the Company?

The modern corporation is, indeed, a child of the East

India Company and there is much to learn from the mother's failures and successes. In its extraordinary history lie answers to the great questions faced by business people throughout history—how to mitigate risk, raise capital, build trust with customers and suppliers, motivate employees, keep shareholders happy and achieve a harmonious relationship with society.

The Company was one of the pioneers of the shareholder or joint-stock model of corporate enterprise. As an early joint-stock company it derived huge competitive advantage—it could mobilize vast amounts of capital and operate on a much bigger scale than before. By separating investors from the professional managers who ran the business, it achieved a division of labour that made it more efficient. Unlike the 'owner' or 'partner' model of business, it was able to distribute risk widely—it shielded shareholders from losses as they were only responsible up to the value of their paid-up capital. Since it was a 'legal person', it could act independently beyond the interests of its investors. Indeed, the corporate form of doing business is one of the reasons for the rise of the West in the transition from the pre-modern to the modern periods in history (and possibly the backwardness of other societies such as the Islamic Middle East, as argued by some scholars).

The English got the concept of a corporation from

Roman law—in particular, the ideas of a legal personality, limited liability and variable shareholdings. The Italians in the fifteenth century experimented with the corporate form during the flowering of their great multinational business houses, such as the Medicis of Florence (although it was in the city of Genoa that public loans were first used to finance companies). In sixteenth-century England, chartered companies brought together a group of merchants, seamen, adventurers and politicians in order to buy and sell goods on a common platform. The idea of pooling resources, however, went back to the medieval guild—a commercial body of merchants who made rules for trade and formed part of town administration. The chartered companies took great risks to finance sea voyages over vast distances which sometimes took years; their capital costs were high and the ships carried high-value luxuries, as well as gold and silver to pay for them. Everything could be lost in a storm. Hence, spreading the shareholding and the backing of the state helped to mitigate risk.

As one of the earliest corporations, the Company evolved a hierarchical model of management that is still followed by today's multinational companies. Its commercial success also lay in its information management system, not unlike today. Whereas it matched supply and demand through an army of 'writers' and clerks, today's marketing professionals achieve the same thing through highly sophisticated software. But even the best of information depends, in the end, on a 'feel for the market'. The Company's directors debated the same sort of issues—for example, how do you balance headquarters control with autonomy of the local subsidiary—that multinational companies wrestle with today. These are some of its enduring legacies for business enterprises today.

The major difference between the Company and the modern corporation is that it was a monopoly created by the state, privileged by a charter granted by the Crown (later by Parliament) because it was thought to have a public purpose as well as private interest. Such chartered companies have largely disappeared—the BBC is one of the few that remain—as the modern age has rebelled against the notion of monopoly. Today in our democratic times anyone literally can start a company and raise capital by listing it on the stock exchange. And its share price is dependent far more on vigorous competitive forces, unlike chartered companies, whose monopoly powers were able to maintain high share prices.

Gradually, in the eighteenth century, public sentiment in Britain turned against the idea of a monopoly chartered by the government that furthered private interest. This was partly due to the misdeeds of the Company, but in fact, the coming of the Industrial Revolution with its vigorously competitive and innovative companies made the idea obsolete. In today's jargon, the Company had acquired the unacceptable odour of 'crony capitalism'. Soon it became an anachronism and when it died in 1874, the era of the chartered corporation died with it.

Public monopolies did not die, however. They were popular around the world during 'socialist periods' of the twentieth century. The post-Independence government of India between 1956 and 1981, in a period popularly called 'License Raj', was as biased in favour of public monopoly and against private enterprise as the mercantile state in Europe. These state monopolies were beset with some of the problems that Adam Smith had forecast: poor customer service, high costs, weak profits, poor work ethic among employees, poor capital output ratios and low accountability.

Business is based on trust far more than on contract

Underlying Tirthankar Roy's persuasive narrative is the moral idea of trust. Although Indian and the Company merchants did not often like each other, they ultimately built a relationship based on self interest, and this usually entailed sticking to one's word. As the scale of operations expanded, the Company's buying system in India evolved from 'spot purchases' in the bazaar to 'long term contracts'. Since there were no courts to enforce contracts, both sides depended on the other's integrity. Sometimes the trust was breached. And power also mattered—the merchants of Surat were able to better protect their interests when Mughal authority over Surat was stronger. But the best officers of the Company recognized that long-term success depended on the confidence that its word and its name generated—much as a 'brand name' does in the contemporary world.

In the same way, Indian agents or 'banias' built a reputation for which they were rewarded with repeat business and some went on to become large houses that carried on for generations. Trust allowed a financier to take vast risks with large amounts of cash through instruments such as the hundi, a promissory note payable on demand in a far-flung city. Trust usually began in a joint family, or the sub-caste, but it had to inevitably extend to strangers as business grew. Trade entails transactions with outsiders, often foreigners. Over time repeated actions of a certain kind build confidence and are an invitation for partnerships.

The Company's corporate form also helped to create trust. Customers and suppliers found they were dealing with an institution which would outlive the whims of an individual. Potential employees thought they were joining an institution of professionals rather than an individual or a family. The joint-stock structure created trust among shareholders as their liability would be limited in a disaster. Military and political power was obviously important to the Company's long-term success, but it was its ability to generate trust with customers, suppliers and shareholders that allowed it to endure commercially for more than two centuries.

Tirthankar Roy reminds us that Indian and European merchants did not usually become friends, which suggests that business relationships depend far more on mutual trust rather than friendship. However, the ability to become friends does give one a competitive advantage—the decline of old British firms in the 1920s and 1930s and the rise of multinationals is connected to the latter's superior ability to relate to Indians, as Maria Misra has argued. As the Company's political power expanded, the English went on to establish modern courts in the territories under their control for enforcing commercial contracts. Formal courts brought greater predictability to business life as business actors felt reassured that contracts were backed by the power of the judiciary and the police. This is one of the reasons for the amazing success of the port cities of Bombay,

Calcutta and Madras. Merchants and bankers migrated to these cities for many reasons (mostly commercial) but one of them was the increasing rule of commercial law.

Since there are almost no records of Indian business firms before the Company made its appearance, it is difficult to know how traditional contracts were enforced in pre-modern India. Roy suggests that traditional contracts were more useful for collecting debt than to enforce conditions of sales. The dharmashastra has an entire section called vyavahara, 'transactions', or vivada, 'disputes', which suggests the presence of some kind of court for civil disputes, that included matters of payment for goods, disagreement of partners, disputes about wages and the like. There are indeed records of various sorts of merchant courts and chief merchants—the Nagar Seth, for example, which had parallels in other parts of India.

The larger point I am making, however, is that despite contracts and courts, business transactions, both then and now, are based on good faith between human beings. Edward Banfield illustrated this in his classic, *The Moral Basis of a Backward Society*. He attributed the relative failure of South Italy to the absence of trust outside the family versus higher levels of trust towards non-family members in the more prosperous North Italy. The legal contract is thus only a last resort. This has always been true and continues to be so in the vigorous global economy of the twenty-first century when daily transactions in the billions of dollars depend on trust.

Monopoly, corporate governance and Adam Smith

Adam Smith's disgust at the monopoly of the East India Company partly drove the famous Scottish philosopher to write his great work, *An Enquiry into the Nature and Causes of the Wealth of Nations,* the foundational text of capitalism. Smith published it in 1776 at the height of the attack on the Company by Edmund Burke, Sheridan, Lord North and many Members of Parliament.

In his book, Smith concludes that monopoly is bad for everyone—consumers, suppliers, employees and society as a whole. It destroys the foundation of the market as competition is necessary to discipline and regulate the self-interested behaviour of individuals. He argues in the *Wealth of Nations* for an 'obvious and simple system of natural liberty' in which the pursuit of self-interest is guided by 'an invisible hand' which benefits the whole society and raises its standards of living.

Although the East India Company's monopoly status

was 'an unjustified tax on both consumers and producers', according to Adam Smith, the reality was that the Company faced considerable competition from the private trade of its own employees. A fundamental flaw in the compensation structure of its employees allowed many to carry on business on the side, and some became hugely wealthy as a result. Corporate executives today are able to become wealthy (via stock options, for example) but no corporation would allow competition with itself. Even then the Company was constantly uncomfortable with it and tried to ban it periodically. It tried to prosecute its most outstanding employees—Oxenden, Aungier, Day, Yale. Roy tells us that the most notorious employee-competitor was Thomas Pitt who returned home with a great fortune, including one of the world's largest diamonds, which eventually went on to adorn Marie Antoinette's crown and Napoleon's sword. Pitt went to acquire a seat in Parliament from where he attacked the Company's monopoly.

But Adam Smith found a different flaw. Private trade of the Company's employees confirmed to him a fundamental defect in the joint-stock company, where ownership was separated from management. He worried that employees might turn the corporation to their own ends and not look after shareholders' interests with the 'same anxious vigilance' that an owner or a partner would and, as a result, 'negligence and profusion must always prevail, more or less, in the management of the affairs of such a company'. Smith's was a prescient warning. Even today audit committees of company boards are wrestling with accountability of executives to shareholders. While separation of owners and managers has many positives—the ability to source capital from a wide range of investors and replace incompetent children of hereditary founders by effective professionals—the limited liability of shareholders makes for carelessness in the oversight of funds and leaves a company vulnerable to executive malpractice. The standards of governance are obviously higher today but there remains an ever present danger of executives exploiting the corporation for their own ends, just as the Company's executives did in the eighteenth century.

The attack on the Company's monopoly grew over time in which Adam Smith was often quoted. Its share price boomed when news of the acquisition of the Bengal diwani from the Mughal emperor reached London's financial markets in April 1766. However, the Bengal Bubble burst soon afterwards on repeated bad news about mismanagement in India. Many Members of Parliament were shareholders and, as the stock price plunged, they grew angry. There were cries against the

Company's monopoly and this led to the reforms of the 1770s, 1780s and 1790s, which effectively punctured the Company's autonomy as a business and breached its monopoly.

By the beginning of the nineteenth century, the Company went into decline as a commercial concern. It was partly due its political troubles with Parliament, but had more to do with Britain's industrial revolution which changed the pattern of trade. Consumers in England were now happy with cheaper cottons from their own mills and the Company's famous auctions of Indian cottons declined precipitously. Weavers in India could not compete with machine-made cloth. If the Company had not been rescued by the growing trade with China in tea and opium, it would have quickly died. Its commercial importance declined in India after the 1820s where it essentially became a political administrator until the British government officially took over India after 1857.

The Company's second fortune

The Company made its 'second fortune' in China. Since Roy's book is confined to India, I shall supplement it with some remarks on its Chinese personality. The English love affair with Chinese tea began to grow after

Parliament passed Pitt's Commutation Act of 1784 which lowered barriers to the entry of tea and undercut smuggling. Consumption grew steadily and the Company's profits from tea auctions touched a £1 million a year by 1833. Its second fortune was financed initially by silver bullion, but gradually it was funded by opium.

The Celestial Empire of Qing China disliked foreigners and refused to trade with Europeans as it would have implied equality and compromised its sense of superiority. The Company persevered, however, and eventually set up temporary trade facilities in Canton on the Pearl River. There it found its match in a cartel of Chinese merchants, the Co-Hong, who inflicted constant humiliation. China was the only source of tea and even arrogant monopolies learn to bend. Gradually the two monopolies began to trust each other—to the point that Co-Hong accepted the Company's word for the number of tea chests that failed quality control in London.

So millions of pounds of tea began to pass through the Company's warehouses in Canton. The most popular varieties were four black teas—Bohea, Congo, Souchon and Pekoe—and three green teas—Singlo, Heyson and Bing. The tea travelled west on the Company's ships to Britain and beyond. On the return journey, the ships picked up silver to pay for the tea. The huge export of silver created a balance-of-payments problem for Britain. In India, the answer to this problem had been Clive and after that the Industrial Revolution. But in China the Company became a drug-lord and reversed the flow of bullion by selling high-quality Patna opium. It encouraged peasants in Bihar and Bengal to cultivate opium, which it smuggled through third parties into China in chests branded with Company seals (chaap).

As opium was illegal in China, the Company's ships could not carry it. So it sold it in auctions in Calcutta from where it made its way to China. The drug was smuggled by independent agents, such as Jardine Matheson and Dent & Co., who established an intricate network of bribes at the Chinese customs (hoppo) who turned a blind eye to the contraband. The proceeds of the smuggled drug were deposited with the Company's factory at Canton. By 1825, most of the funds needed to buy tea in China were raised through opium.

So successful was the poppy crop that its growing rapidly expanded to central and western India, especially the Malwa territories of the Marathas, from where it was exported to Macao via Bombay. There were many reasons for the Maratha Wars and the control of opium trade was one of them. In 1838, when smuggled opium approached an amazing 1400 tons a year, the Chinese imposed the death penalty for opium smuggling and sent a Special Imperial Commissioner, Lin Zexu, to curb smuggling. This led to the First Opium War (1839–42) between China and Britain. China lost and had to cede Hong Kong to Britain under the Treaty of Nanking. A Second Opium War was fought by Britain and France against China from 1856 until 1860. China lost again.

In the end, opium trade did great damage to China. According to some accounts 27 per cent of Chinese males in the 1870s were seriously addicted and in 1905, one in five males in China was reportedly an opium smoker. Millions suffered and died of addiction in the nineteenth century, which the Chinese call a 'century of humiliation'. Only in 1907 did Britain finally agree to stop the export of Indian opium, and in 1911 its manufacture was abandoned in Bihar. It was Mao's revolution in 1948, however, which finally cured China of its opium addiction.

The importance of being the East India Company

Thomas Babington Macaulay, the English historian, essayist and politician, called the East India Company 'the greatest corporation in the world'. Today we would not use those words. We might call it the world's most 'powerful' corporation, which it was during its 275-year life that extended from the mercantilist period of chartered monopolies to the industrial age of the modern corporation. We might also think about its tragic nature which created so much wealth but also did much damage. The East India Company's story is a cautionary tale about the dangers of monopoly but it is also an inspiration as the pioneer of many corporate institutions that are a part of our modern world.

Mercifully, as Tirthankar Roy points out, corporations do not invade countries today. It is a long way from 1612 when the Company defeated the Portuguese navy off the coast of Surat and won its first trade concession from the Mughal emperor. Legitimate corporations no longer maintain private armies, although security is an obsession with many. Nor do they aspire to become drug lords. The East India Company engaged in violence, drug-dealing and openly bribed Members of Parliament and high officials in exchange for licenses and favours. This is the dark side of the story.

But its institutional contributions are equally impressive. The joint-stock ownership has survived the industrial and the post-industrial ages. So has the hierarchical system of management. The Company did an impressive job of rewarding and motivating employees and creating an environment for careers open to the talented. Roy recounts inspiring stories of many talented young men—Oxenden, Aungier, Charnock and others—who rose from below and went on to perform extraordinary, often heroic, deeds thousands of miles away from home. It is not an accident that the Company managed to throw up talent generation after generation, and gain its loyalty. Although Adam Smith fretted about the moral hazard in separating investors from professional managers, the Company obviously achieved efficiency through the division of labour. Smith may have been distrustful of employees but the Company's shareholders were not. This innovation survives, although boards of companies still wrestle with the issues of corporate governance that Smith raised about the accountability of employees in a faceless setup.

Monopoly was clearly a birth defect, but it was constantly breached and it created a flawed corporate culture which led to conflict in the minds of its employees between private and corporate interest. The Company had permitted private trade in the belief that employees were not sufficiently compensated for the huge risks involved. It soon realized its mistake, however, and tried to stamp it out—but without success. Companies today reward employees for taking great risks, but they do so in a transparent way through bonuses and stock options, which have the additional benefit of aligning the individual's with the company's goals. Some entrepreneurial communities, such as Marwaris and Jains, have a similar way of compensating employees—allowing them to trade privately. Often, however, it is a method of training youngsters who in a few years are expected to set out on their own.

Every child in India grows up reading in school the perfidious story of how Clive and the Company stole Bengal at Plassey in 1757. So, it is hardly surprising that Indians remain suspicious of trade, merchants and foreign companies. 'The return of the East India Company' is still invoked in public discourse about trade liberalization, multinationals and market-based policies. More than sixty years after Independence, India has become the world's second-fastest growing economy, the minds of the young are decolonized and liberated, and so it is time, perhaps, to get over the 'East India Company syndrome'.

The 'East India Company syndrome' has been behind a sentiment called swadeshi in India's public life after Independence. It is variously nationalist, xenophobic, anti-foreign, and usually exhibits itself in a clamour for tariff protection and self reliance in economic policy. It was first practised with Mahatma Gandhi in the 1920s, who used it successfully as a political tool to mobilize

Indians against foreign rule. But after Independence, it was exploited by businessmen to get barriers erected against foreign goods and investment. The economic reforms of the 1990s were a clear turning point against this sentiment as tariff walls tumbled and India opened up to trade and investment despite rearguard action by the protectionist Bombay Club.

Tirathankar Roy's story of the East India Company has brought a fresh perspective to history, which for too long has been a dreary account of the reign of kings. He breathes life into history, as will the rest of the volumes in our series, in creating a romantic, adventurous world of seafaring merchants who took mad risks; of highly skilled craftsmen who made beautiful products; of bankers who provided capital which sometimes bankrupted them; and rulers who realized from time to time that their self interest lay in nurturing business.

Gurcharan Das

PREFACE

I AM INDEBTED to Huw Bowen, Gurcharan Das, Om Prakash, Lakshmi Subramanian and Thomas R. Trautmann, who read previous versions of the text with great care and patience, and offered detailed, insightful and valuable comments. The comments led to numerous editorial and stylistic changes, correction of errors, fresh reading, extensions, and sometimes restatement of the arguments. Thanks are also due to Sanjay Subrahmanyam for suggesting important references.

I need to clarify two stylistic points. In order to keep the text unburdened with footnotes, I have refrained from adding citation details in the text, except to mention the name of the author and sometimes the date of publication, if relevant to the context. Full details of the work can be found in the bibliography at the end of the book. Throughout the text, the names of the three Company towns (Bombay, Calcutta and Madras) follow the old convention.

INTRODUCTION

BUSINESS AND POLITICS were transformed in South Asia between 1600 and 1800. The English East India Company was one of the main agents of the change. In these two centuries, the Company created a mass market in Britain for Asian goods, including Indonesian spices, Indian cotton cloth and Chinese tea. It created new channels of intra-Asian trade, bringing Persia, India, China and Indonesia closer than ever before. The Company established three port cities in India which drew wealthy and skilled people from all over India. It converted vast quantities of American silver into Asian goods. And the Company was the means by which European colonialism in South Asia began. Not only was it pivotal in India, it enjoyed similar importance in Britain as well. At its peak, the Company was the most important mercantile firm in London, wielding political influence and commanding large financial resources. There was hardly any prominent figure in the business world of London in these two centuries who did not take an interest in the Company or was not connected with it.

Written about extensively, the Company remains an enigma to historians. A firm enjoying a state guaranteed monopoly, it was also an umbrella for private enterprise conducted by its own employees. Started with the express intention of trading in the Indian Ocean, it gradually transformed itself into a colonial power. British in origin, the Company's mercantile choices were shaped by current conventions of business in Asia. Ambitions of partners and agents, individuals who ran its operations overseas, the Indian kings and nobles with whom it had to negotiate the right to trade, and the political disputes in which the Company got embroiled in, had to be factored in while trading. The East India Company became an entity with many faces, of which the imperial one eventually came to overshadow the others.

How do we explain this baffling phenomenon of a peddler of goods transforming itself into a world power? The task would become easier if we could answer two significant questions. One of these is a question of origin and the other one is a question of definition. Why did a transnational corporate firm, a rare entity in the seventeenth century, appear in Western Europe rather than in the other prominent commercial regions of the contemporary world, India or China, for example? As to the question of definition—what kind of an entity was the East India Company? How similar or different was it from the modern firm?

If the question of origin demands no more than a straightforward narrative, it is the definition of 'Company' that raises peculiar difficulties. Most histories of trade and empire in the early modern world suggest that the Company's territorial conquests cannot be understood as results of accident or opportunism, but were connected with the very character of the organization itself. If there is any truth in this, the Company must have been a very different body from what we would understand today by the term 'company'. Surely today's multinationals do not, at least not all of them, feel obliged to invade the countries where they do business in? On the other hand, the prospect that the Company succeeded as a business venture thanks to its organizational form, should invite us to compare the Company then with companies now in the hope of finding some similarity between them. From current perspective, it would be interesting to know what differentiates business objectives and strategies of the East India Company from those of today's multinational conglomerates.

Viewed in another way, in studying the East India Company, we study an organization that simultaneously served profit and power. In performing this task, it will not be enough to restrict our attention to rules of business and economics alone. We need to merge them with the rules of politics. This is a complex undertaking, but one that gives the Company story its peculiar attraction.

Origin

The East India Company was formed in London on the last day of 1600 by a group of merchants, mariners, explorers and politicians. Its mandate was to finance trading voyages to India, Southeast Asia and China with subscribed capital.

The desire to trade overseas, and sponsor merchant fleets for the purpose, had been a long-standing one, and took shape in response to the rise of the Iberian empire in America and Portuguese power in the Indian Ocean. Approximately a century before the Company started, Vasco Da Gama, Alvarez Cabral and Aphonso de Albuquerque had established a Portuguese sphere of influence on the western coast of India. Da Gama discovered the passage to India and Southeast Asia via the Cape of Good Hope. The sea route was long and dangerous with the risk of violent tropical storms near the Cape. The journey across the Arabian Sea was unfamiliar to many sailors, and required taking on board Indian navigators from the east African port of Zanzibar. The sea route was none the less an important discovery because it allowed the Europeans access to the east without having to go overland or across West Asia, which would mean negotiating passage with potentially hostile powers like the Caliph of Egypt, the Ottoman Turks and the Shah of Persia. The Mediterranean route to the east, furthermore, was monopolized by Venetian and Genoese merchants. As the Portuguese established posts and colonies in Diu, Bassein, Ceylon and Goa, their hegemony on the seas was constantly challenged by the maritime states on the Arabian Sea littoral. But these threats were not very serious ones.

The economic interest of the Portuguese in this time lay much further east, in the spices from the Indonesian islands. Eastern spices sold at astronomical profits in the markets of Europe. A successful trading enterprise could bring goods capable of making a 1000 per cent profit, justifying constant threat from piracy, tropical storm, shipwreck and attacks by rivals. The spices, moreover, could be paid for with other goods from the east, such as cotton cloth from India, which were cheap and in demand everywhere. It is difficult to imagine that such profit opportunities would go uncontested for long. In the mid-sixteenth century, coinciding with the reign of Elizabeth I in England, the challenge to the Portuguese supremacy in the east began to take shape in England and Holland. These two Protestant powers looked at the Catholic nations of Spain and Portugal as political and economic rivals. But it was not only the religious rivalry, nor the profit motive, insecurity and royal patronage, that can explain the outburst of maritime enterprise that followed in the next decades.

Elizabethan London represented a unique conjunction of elements to make a maritime revolution likely. Sailors, soldiers, landlords, artisans, scientists, artists and merchants—ordinary people all and divided one from the other by class barriers—shared a curiosity about Asia. In a uniquely English fashion, groups in command of diverse skills came together to serve the common purpose of exploration of that world.

In the later decades of the sixteenth century, dramatic episodes of maritime exploration led by Walter Raleigh, Humphrey Gilbert, John Hawkins and Martin Frobisher had taken place. In the course of these voyages, nautical instruments like astrolabes and the compass were perfected, and knowledge about navigation tools, maps and charts, and oceanic currents had travelled from China and the Mediterranean to Western Europe.

Around the same time, the average size of ships built on the Thames increased considerably, and the English could match their nautical and naval capacity as well as knowledge of the seas with that of the Dutch, the Spanish and the Portuguese.

Curious and brilliant scientific minds joined the adventurers. The greatest of them perhaps was 'Dr' John Dee, Cambridge-schooled mathematician, explorer and consultant to some of the leading contemporary expeditions, including those led by Martin Frobisher to Canada. He had financial stake in several of the ventures into the New World, and his theoretical knowledge of navigation was constantly drawn upon by leading mariners. An amateur astrologer, he prepared the horoscopes of sea captains, and considering how many sea captains made it big, must have been good at telling fortunes. Dee, it is said, coined the term 'British Empire', meaning territories in the northern hemisphere that were subjugated during King Arthur's mythical conquests in the sixth century, and to which the British Crown could legitimately lay claim.

A confidence in the ability to conduct hazardous journeys joined hands with the money that came in from a coterie of merchants of the City of London. In the beginning of Elizabeth's reign in 1558, the City merchants were only a few hundred in number, the majority among them belonging to the cloth merchants' guild. Forty years later, business had grown and the numbers were larger. The Crown's own income was never enough to maintain the expensive navy. Hence, potential income from trade and contributions of the merchants were becoming attractive options for the state. The Queen's order to expel the Hanseatic League of merchants from England in 1597 led to a shifting of English commercial capital from the Continent to England, and saw a more ambitious and outward-looking class deciding affairs in the City. For many of the merchants who had been to the Continent, a teeming world of commerce with India and China, in which the only Europeans to participate until now had been the Portuguese, seemed almost within reach.

The obstacles to successful maritime expeditions in Asia were many. Quite apart from the physical hazards of the journeys, there was the rivalry with the Iberians. The Portuguese and the Spanish were entrenched in the sea routes to the west and the east, and if the English were to break into the trading world of Asia by sea, they needed to overcome stiff naval challenge from these two nations. During the sixteenth century, expeditions to discover a north-eastern passage to India, which would avoid the Portuguese, were proposed. After much money was spent and several books had been written on the subject, the quest was abandoned as unattainable.

Events of the last decades of the sixteenth century, however, showed the English that the Iberians were not invincible. Indeed at times surprisingly poorly defended in the Atlantic. The Spanish and the Portuguese had overstretched themselves in trying to control open seas with very limited resources. While trying to protect a maritime monopoly, they had neglected trade. Consequently, the wealth of their colonies had not risen in line with territorial ambitions. In the Spanish case the colonies would soon be draining the mother country.

That these powers could be defeated was tellingly demonstrated by the great 'pirate' Francis Drake. In the 1560s, Drake built his career by raiding Spanish treasure trains in the Panama isthmus, and sending the loot home. These raids also gave him possession of ships captured from the Spaniards, and in turn, brought him the status of merchant. His daring and ruthlessness made him an ideal candidate to lead an ambitious enterprise to raid Spanish possessions in the Pacific, sponsored by a number of 'equall companions and frindly gentlemen', among whom was included the Queen herself. Drake's dramatic exploits on the Pacific coast of South America capturing one ship after another exposed the weakness and unpreparedness of the Spanish naval presence. Along with much gold and silver, these raids yielded a cluster of maps that eventually helped Drake cross the Pacific itself. In 1588, Drake and other commanders orchestrated the defeat of the greatest fleet in Europe, the Spanish Armada. Drake's Pacific journey was closely followed by another under Thomas Cavendish.

Unlike trips to the Atlantic and the Pacific, which were primarily for territorial control, the Indian Ocean expeditions of the West European nations were motivated mainly by the prospect of commercial profits though they had to reckon with Portuguese resistance. When the West Europeans ventured into Asian trade, they formed a mercantile company. It was this organizational innovation, as well as the propensity to trade overseas, that distinguished the English and other Europeans at this time from the Indians or the Chinese.

The meaning of a 'company'

Although long-distance trade was not more developed in Europe than Asia, the company form of organization, together with monopoly charter and the backing of the king were unique features of commerce in western Europe and had no counterpart in the Asian business tradition. Partly reflecting this institutional ability of pooling large amounts of money together, interest rates were lower in western Europe than in India.

Interest rates in India were generally much higher, but when lenders and borrowers were linked by caste and kinship, the rates came down. Therefore, organized enterprise that involved much risk and large capital tended to be confined to castes and communities, between the members of which there was sufficient trust. Interest rates did not ordinarily need to cover the risk of default when lending was done between a father and a son, or an uncle and a nephew. For most large trading or banking firms in early modern India, principals and agents tended to belong in the same caste or community. Both were merchants, often related by blood and marriage, and had similar commercial interests, ambitions and capacities.

The English association or corporate firm was an alternative to this, Asian, organizational model. Like the community, it was founded on common interest, but unlike the community, it did not stand on a foundation of ethnic and filial loyalties. It was potentially more unstable in the short run than a family. The ambitions of the principals and the agents were not perfectly matched. But it was a more powerful, and therefore stable, entity in the long run than a family. It was more powerful because it could embrace innovative yet risky ideas more readily than could a community, being unencumbered by family ties; and it was more stable because it could change with the times. The association form allowed the company to consider financing maritime expeditions that involved uncertainty, whereas the Indian merchants were known for their risk-averse mentalities.

The association form lowered the entry bar to private enterprise for all kinds of wealthy people, and thus enabled a collaboration to develop between diverse forms of capability. The decision to put money into expeditions seemed sensible to many rich Londoners precisely because such enterprises depended for their success upon collaboration between navigation and commercial skills. The company form could more easily create conditions for such collaboration. The one singular element of the English context, therefore, without which the Company's origin cannot be understood, is the partnership between merchants-bankers and sailors-soldiers-navigators. Of course, merchants routinely hired sailors and soldiers in India too. But sailors persuading merchants to take unique patterns of commercial risk —precisely what led to the founding of the Company— would be a very unusual phenomenon in contemporary India. On the point of enabling an equal partnership between navigators and merchants, Western Europe in 1600 had become an exceptional corner of the world, even though the merchants hardly had any idea where that exceptionality might lead them.

In addition, the adoption of joint-stock and limited liability gave the Company a specifically modern form.

Origins of the joint stock

The origin of the joint-stock company is attributed variously to the medieval partnerships in England, German corporatism and a Genovese institution of raising a public loan to finance a company. The Genovese institution in turn derived from an Arabic root. The significance of these forms derived from the use made of them by the guild merchants of the towns and boroughs. The guilds were a part of the town administration, which regulated the right of its members to practice a trade. In principle, the guild needed a constitution to ensure that only the lawful members had access to the profits of trade. The legal aspect demanded some form of administrative charter or license, so that law-breakers could be punished by the state. In England, the Crown had the power by common law to grant charters of incorporation to associations of merchants. The chartered rights thus awarded followed a common template; and a common set of rights and duties applied to all of the overseas trading companies as well.

In the sixteenth century, commercial bodies that had originated in the guilds were beginning to move out of the towns in their immediate vicinity to distant port cities for greater business opportunities. One of the earliest expressions of the guilds venturing out was the formation of the London firm, Company of Merchant Adventurers, in 1505 to counter growth of trade in the Flanders. In order to achieve this, such firms needed to empower the overseas chief with some law-enforcement privileges. From 'regulated' companies where the collectively held wealth was liable for losses, these trading companies gradually transformed themselves into joint-stock ventures with limited liability. The application of the limited liability principle enabled larger flows of savings into shareholding, as William Scott showed in a classic treatise on corporate law.

The royal charters issued between 1580 and 1610 in response to applications from merchants seeking profits overseas inherited their constitution from the guilds. And not unlike the town guild, they were all charters to create monopolies. The overseas chartered company sought and received the privilege to exclude other countrymen from overseas trade in a specific area. But this monopoly was unlike any other. Unlike the towns, the oceans did not have a government of their own, and presented logistical difficulty of enforcing any monopoly.

The overseas charter, therefore, was in practice contestable.

In the specific case of the East India Company, the moral right to a monopoly came under constant attack. The Company managed to keep shareholding restricted, so that the monopoly profits accrued to a few. The conjunction of profit and privilege made groups within the Parliament contend that its charter was in breach of basic rights of freedom. Private traders or 'interlopers' from the early 1600s sought the backing of these lobbies. The sentiment did see rival companies form, but a formal end to the charter did not happen until 1813. For one thing, the ideological opposition was divided. Some among those who opposed monopoly in domestic trade still favoured monopoly in overseas trade. For another, the opposition was more or less confined to merchants. A truly universal critique of monopoly had to await Adam Smith's *Wealth of Nations* (1776).

Until then, the criticism of the Company was slow to develop, and was bred by its very success. The critics were well aware that the monopoly charter had been instrumental in the making of its fortune. The commercial-maritime enterprise entailed great financial and physical risks. In the early 1600s, possibly half of those who set out to go overseas died from scurvy, storms, pirate attacks and shipwrecks. Goods brought from India or the Indonesian islands to England or Holland were expensive luxuries that sold in markets susceptible to economic shocks or epidemic attacks. Capital was needed to maintain an elaborate infrastructure of factory, fort, sailors, ships and soldiers. The business of overseas trade could weather these risks only if it was unusually profitable and run on a very large scale. The monopoly charter helped it earn large profits and the joint stock provided the scale.

In turn, the early Company brought to India an organizational principle that had been rare in the region's economic and political tradition. It sought a royal charter from an Indian king. And it sent the most able diplomats to discuss the terms. In order to maintain the level of sophistication in negotiation, the chiefs of the Company's distant outposts tended to be senior merchants. Negotiation skill became a benchmark with which individual ability in the Company's hierarchy would be assessed, and young men could move up quickly based on this ability. Learning an Indian language helped as it could facilitate direct communication with the Indians.

In this fashion, there emerged the characteristic form of the Western European chartered companies trading in Asia.

Conflict of interest

It is sometimes suggested that the chartered companies were the precursors of the modern joint-stock company. This is true only in a narrow sense. The differences were fundamental. There were two main differences.

Firstly, the Company was formed during a time when shareholding by the public, and professional management, were still unknown. The identity of the Company was hardly distinct from the identity of the owners. Even when the shares were traded widely, the Company never acquired an identity independent of the oligarchy of the largest shareholders who controlled all policy matters. Secondly, whereas the term 'company' would evoke today the picture of an organization where the employees work for the interests of the shareholders and under a central command centre, the East India Company was an enterprise in which the head did not have perfect control over the limbs. This lack of control was deliberate. The very design of personnel management made the overseas branches somewhat autonomous from the head office.

The formation and functioning of the Company can be read as a partnership between the sedentary bankers and merchants of the City of London and the peripatetic sailors and soldiers. The merchants supplied the money, the sailors navigated the waters, and the soldiers ensured security. Merchants and soldiers, the smooth and the rough sides of society, hailed from different classes, had different world views, and did not share an innate propensity to become friends. If the partnership were to work, profits of the enterprise had to be shared, or the sailors and soldiers allowed to trade on their own account. The Company paid them small salaries, but allowed them limited scope for private trade.

The scope to pursue private interest while working for a firm imparted an element of instability on the whole enterprise. The tendency to develop a split personality was intrinsic to the constitution of the Company. The individuals could trade too much and step into the Company's preserves. They often built subsidiary partnerships with merchants, artisans and powerful individuals at the trade sites, which could overstep limits of social or political engagement set by their employers and principals. The Company directors ordinarily had a set of incentive and punishment systems in place to make the employees desist from crossing the boundaries. On some occasions, however, the Company directors were either powerless to prevent them, or preferred to wait and watch, nervously stepping in when things had gone too far.

The backing of the Crown drove the wedge between the head office and the branches even further. The overseas branch could claim to be acting in the interest of the monarch, when some of its decisions were disputed by the head office. The royal charter was indirectly an endorsement of mercantile law or regulation. Another aspect of the charter, which gained significance over time due to European warfare in the late seventeenth and eighteenth century, was the offer of arms for the use of maritime trade. Such support was not always used or available when necessary, but its presence, even in theory, changed the character of the trading firm. A part of the sovereign authority to wage war, make laws, and police subjects, was delivered to the chartered companies to enable them to withstand attacks by competitors and predatory states. The historian Julia Adams uses the term 'patrimonial' state to explain this dimension of multinational firms in the early modern world.

Interestingly, the backing of the monarch empowered the overseas branches relatively more than it did the head office, for after all, it was the branch office that had to fight the wars. At times, it may have been easy to convince the head office that warfare and politics were necessary for commerce. But even when the principals thought warfare was unnecessary and unprofitable, the semi-autonomous position in which the agents found themselves, coupled with their own private interests and ambitions, could still spur them on to military engagements.

The bigger problem with sovereign interference was that the Indians also followed a similar political paradigm. With numerous mini-kings, fiefs and vassals, disagreements escalated quickly into battles, especially since there was neither a law book, nor a supreme authority to settle such quarrels.

From merchants to kingmakers

Adam Smith rightly observed that the big difference between the Spanish conquest of the Americas and the English conquest of India was that, in the latter territories, the Europeans encountered powerful states reliant on the support of merchants and landlords. The local officers and tax collectors functioned as law-makers, especially near the coasts. A trade license taken from the imperial court in Agra did not necessarily provide immunity from meddlesome local lords in Surat, Patna or Kasimbazar. If the foreign traders saw themselves as mini-sovereigns, so did the local kings, as did even some of their merchant allies. More fundamentally, the monopoly charter may have been of advantage to the Company, but it was an embarrassment for an Indian king, who received requests of accommodation, and money, from competing merchant bodies all the time and often did not know who to please. In such a situation, disputes over trade licenses, taxation, territorial control and profit-sharing could go out of control, unless settled by means of bribes. In the course of dealing with the local situation, which the London employers did not fully understand, the employees stationed overseas realized that it was too dangerous to behave like obedient servants of London. But if they were not servants of London, they were not subjects of the Indian kings either. Who were their masters, then? It was partly in this ambiguity that the prospect of an empire lay hidden.

Responding to the ambiguity, the overseas branches tried to secure their own military identity in defiance of London, and with this goal in mind founded three mini-kingdoms of their own—Bombay, Madras and Calcutta—by the end of the seventeenth century. In the beginning of their history, these settlements were no more than well-defended villages. They lacked good harbours (Madras had none), were poorer in resources relative to some of the older European settlements such as Surat or Masulipatnam, and constantly in fear of attacks by enemies. But in the eighteenth century, as wars broke out in the interior, these port towns grew by attracting migrant merchants and artisans. By the mid-eighteenth century, the Company's estate was to grow beyond these towns, and include large Mughal provinces. And by 1803, an empire was within sight. Neither the Crown nor the Company's London office had actually planned an empire. And yet an empire happened. Why did it happen? The ambiguous position of the overseas branches provides one part of an answer.

A fuller answer to the question, however, requires us to understand also the unfolding conditions of business in mid-eighteenth century India.

The Europeans and the world of Indian business

The business world that evolved as a result of European presence in Indian markets was essentially a hybrid. It could not be otherwise, given that the Europeans operated in a world that was already adept at long-distance trade and had well-developed institutional conventions. Which elements in the conventions of Indo-European trade were distinctively European and which ones distinctively Indian, is not an easy question to answer. It was of course the case that the joint stock form was previously unknown in India. But this fact did not seem to make an impression upon the leading Indian businesses, who continued to function within family firms with community support. Two other ingredients of European commercial success did, however, make a deep impression on the Indian merchants who collaborated with the Europeans. These were the efficient use of naval power and fortification as a bulwark for trade, and the availability of a framework of formal commercial contracts, enforceable by the state. Neither of these elements was indigenous. The coasts and the ports were not a major military priority for most Indian states before, and commercial contracts had existed at best as unwritten social conventions before. The fullest play of these elements can be seen in the three port cities that the English owned, which made them especially attractive for entrepreneurial Indians. As states grew weaker around them, the merchants and bankers migrated to the Company territories, and increasingly made use of the English commercial law in force in these territories.

On the other hand, in recruiting the Indian partners and agents, the Company and the private traders needed to be mindful of social conventions of castes and communities, and needed to integrate indigenous skills, commercial acumen, capital and leadership structure into the businesses that they ran. The middleman or the agent was a crucial actor, and enjoyed much freedom and power as a result of the extent to which the Europeans had to depend on the agent. In turn, the position of these actors in their own societies was enhanced by association with such a large firm.

In the last twenty years, historians have suggested that the prospect of an empire lay hidden in the deep mutual dependence that had developed between the English Company, private traders, and Indian merchants. The argument is offered as an alternative to an older view advanced by historians sympathetic to the British rule in India that the Company became an empire because the Indian kingdoms were in a state of collapse, and anarchy ruled all round. The Company needed peace and brought about peace by the force of its own arms. This is valid, if at all, for certain regions of India, especially those which were poor in economic resources. It is not valid for the richest regions of India, where the empire began. Bengal on the eve of the Battle of Plassey in 1757 was not a lawless anarchic state.

The alternative view, offered by Christopher Bayly and others, explains the origin of the British empire by pointing out the congruence of interests between Indian merchants and the Company in India. The collapse of the Mughal empire in the second and the third decades of the eighteenth century had led to a dispersal of commerce, banking, coinage and skilled services to new regional centres. Patna, Benares, Pune, Murshidabad, Hyderabad, or Jaipur, acquired the same level of significance that Lahore, Delhi and Agra had enjoyed before. Regionally rooted moneyed classes emerged. Some of them realized that their own interests would be better served by the European traders than by the bankrupt regional courts. The Company found collaborators who would be willing to accept, even plot, a change of regime. The Company, in this view, fell into an Indian pattern of state formation that had been unfolding for some time. In a less political sense, the regime that came in place has been called the 'Anglo-Bania order' by Lakshmi Subramanian.

It is true that in the late-eighteenth century, when the old Indian states were embroiled in strife and collapse, sections of Indian merchants perceived advantages in forming alliances with the English Company. It is also true that a great deal of Indian money was working for the Company, and vice versa, in the eighteenth century. There was indeed a relationship of deep mutual dependence between the European merchants and their Indian counterparts. And yet, if from this evidence we conclude that there was ordinarily a warm and friendly partnership between the European and the Indian capitalists, we would go too far. The relationship was full of contradictions, and these contradictions should suggest to us another very different drive behind the Empire.

Whatever else the Anglo-Bania order may have been, it was not a model of trust and friendship; quite the opposite in fact. European visitors to India rarely had nice things to say about their Indian partners—the merchants, the weavers and the peasants, though they admired the Indians for their skills. And while many complained of 'the mischief they cause under-hand' (John Henry Grose, 1772), and wrote about the Indians' propensity to employ 'low cunning, stratagem, and deceit' (Thomas Tennant, 1804), few writers went so far as the doctor John Fryer (1670) who called the Indian merchant a 'vermin', 'blood-sucker', 'horse-leech', 'flea', 'worse broker than the Jews', 'an expert in lying, dissembling, and cheating', and a 'map of sordidness'. But even when they were more tempered in tone, the Europeans almost never liked the Indian merchants as individuals, and the sentiment was returned.

There were many reasons behind the uneasy relationship. Business ethics were identical with the customs of castes and communities in India; the Europeans and the Indians shared neither the same customs nor similar levels of motivation to engage in local traditions. It was not as if one of them was more honest than the other; their mental models of good conduct were different. Moreover, while earlier potentials for dispute had been limited because the scale of contractual transactions was smaller, the Europeans expanded the use of long-period contracts, without there being a corresponding development of contract law. The prospect of breach of contracts increased greatly as a result. For example, 'the problem of bad debts', writes the historian Om Prakash in a 1998 book, 'plagued all commodities the Europeans procured in India'. Two economists, Rachel Kranton and Anand Swamy, who have recently studied opium and textile contracts, write, 'enforcement problems appear to be widespread: producers default on advances often by engaging in outside sales, and buyers renege on price commitments often by manipulating quality criteria.'

Distrust on the economic plane was aggravated by a lack of social affiliation. The Indians never admitted the Europeans into their inner circles. Personal friendship between business associates on two sides of the race divide was conspicuously rare. This might seem surprising, when we consider how badly the Europeans needed to form personal ties with the Indians in the seventeenth and eighteenth centuries. The average employee of the Company—a young male, who would spend the best part of his youth in India confined to the factory premises—had no other means of obtaining female companionship than by getting friendly with the

Indians. Many of them did take this road, but the women involved in such partnerships came from the less wealthy classes than the Banias and the Brahmins, and even then, many had to cut off ties with their parental homes due to rigid societal norms. The Europeans' closest business associates in India were, socially speaking, a forbidden territory.

Between the Europeans and the Indians, there was partnership no doubt. But it was a partnership that was backed up neither by contract law nor by social bonding. Being based on nothing more than crude self-interest, it was a recipe for distrust. The relationship between Indian merchants and European merchants, in this way, developed an anarchic fringe. But if the Anglo-Bania order was discordant because of frequent breach of contract and social obstacles to fellow feeling, breach of contract could still fuel the Company's desire to control political power by making it more interested in securing the political means to enforce contracts. The writ that was in force in Bombay, Madras and Calcutta needed to run in all of India to ensure a future for Indo-European business. In other words, a theory of discord supplies an alternative view of colonization just as plausible as the theory of partnership.

Historians are unlikely to reach an agreement on what kind of motivation led to the empire. Amidst discords, many fruitful partnerships did develop. Many Indians did earn the confidence of the Company's representatives. Moreover, the Company itself was an ambiguous entity being pulled in different directions in the mid-eighteenth century. In making the point, I cannot do better than cite the historian Holden Furber. 'The real antithesis,' Furber wrote in 1940, 'is between those who stood to profit from the extension of empire in India and those who had been accustomed to profiting solely through trade, the former group being drawn from every class of English society and the latter consisting of the London merchants, ship-owners and sea captains dominant in the company's courts of proprietors and director.' Between 1690 and 1740, the cleavage was widening, just as the collapse of the Mughal empire supplied the means and the motivations to those who believed that an empire was more profitable than trade.

The scope of the book

In this short history of the Company, the well-known story is retold, but by using an angle of vision somewhat unusual in the historical scholarship on the subject. Many histories have been written about the Company, describing the organization in the context of British politics and expansion. In this book by contrast, the Company is in the main a window into the distinctive globalization that occurred in the Indian subcontinent in the seventeenth and eighteenth centuries. The story suggests that any attempt to deal with Indian business history during this time needs to refer to Europe's own expansion overseas, show how the concept of a firm changed, connect traditional modes of doing business with the modern, Britain with India, India with China, politics with economics, and one empire with another. It indicates the great new profitable opportunities that opened up with European trade in the Indian Ocean, and the large transaction costs that early modern commercialization engendered.

Beyond these general themes, the book is interested in two large questions. How should we explain the transformation of the Company from a trader to an empire-builder, with reference to its own organizational structure and to the opportunities that came its way? Subsequent chapters will illustrate the answer I have hinted at earlier in this chapter, which focuses on the divided nature of the organization. The second question is, what effects did the Company, as a trader and as an empire, impart upon the economy and business organization in India? Again, the answer outlined in this chapter will be embellished as we proceed with the story. The concluding chapter will consider the second question more fully.

Before we get to these themes, it is necessary to recreate the big picture. The story begins with the combination of enterprise and exploration for which Elizabethan London has earned a unique place in global history.

THE VOYAGES

IT IS HARDLY possible to identify the precise moment when the Company as an idea was born. After all, European interest in India had grown from medieval times and for very compelling reasons too. However, the decade before the official inauguration of the firm in 1600 and the decade after this event saw the idea of organized trading voyages to the Indian Ocean reach maturity.

Ralph Fitch

On 12 February 1583, a group of Englishmen sailed from Falmouth on a ship called the Tyger, bound for West Asia. The group included the merchants John Newberry, John Eldred and Ralph Fitch, a jeweller William Leedes, and a painter James Story. Newberry was a merchant-explorer who had two years before undertaken a daring overland trip to Hormuz and back, picking up Arabic on the way. Fitch was a leather merchant, and possibly the most senior member of the party. Eldred was a thirty-one-year old trader in Levantine silks. Newberry, Fitch and Eldred had been close to two shareholders of the English Levant Company. These shareholders part-sponsored the expedition. The Company had been doing business in Constantinople for some years, and brought back samples of cotton cloth from India, silks from China, and spices of the Indonesian archipelago. The goal of the expedition was to explore a way to reach the sources of these goods.

The party reached Tripoli in Syria, crossed the Lebanese mountains to reach Aleppo, and from there sailed along the Euphrates to Al-Fallûjah. At this point Eldred stayed on to trade in spices, and the rest of the group journeyed on to reach Hormuz. Hormuz belonged to the Persian empire, but in practice, the Portuguese ruled this port so vital to their policy of blockading the Indian Ocean routes to all but friendly ships. Their friends, the Venetian merchants, did not want English merchants in West Asia. In a recent contest between the Spanish monarch and a Portuguese nobleman for the Portuguese throne, the English took the nobleman's side and their rivals the Venetian merchants supported the Spanish Crown. Not surprisingly, then, the travellers were promptly arrested at Hormuz. The Portuguese chief justice or aveador-general decided that they were spies, ignoring the letters of introduction they had obtained from Queen Elizabeth, addressed to the emperors of India and China.

The party was sent on a Portuguese galleon to Goa to be interrogated by the viceroy Don Francisco de Mascarenhas. Thirteen days into captivity, Story became a Jesuit, 'partly for feare', and was released. The release of the rest of the group was secured by the intervention of an English Jesuit Thomas Stevens, who was a known figure in Goa. Once freed, the party lost no time setting up business in Goa. However, the Jesuits kept the pressure on to convert them to Catholicism, and allegedly hatched a plot to get them rearrested. Fearing further trouble the party escaped Goa late in 1584.

The group travelled overland to Belgaum, and onward to Bijapur, Burhanpur, Mandu and Ujjain. A few miles away from Ujjain, the party came into a resplendent procession of Emperor Akbar. Early the following year, the group reached Agra. Although the party appeared to have been well received at the court, it is not known if any of these men actually met the emperor to deliver the letter of the Queen to him. The group now divided.

Fitch was to travel to Bengal. Newberry was to go to England over the land route, and return with a ship to Bengal and meet Fitch there. Newberry did set out on the journey, but was not heard of again. Leedes took up service with the Mughal court and never returned to England. The others continued on to 'Bengala', the legendary land that supplied so many finely woven cloths to the markets of west and east Asia.

Fitch went from Agra to Benares, the Bengal port of Saptagram, and navigated through the treacherous waters of the Sundarbans to reach Bakla. Since he does not mention either overland journey or changing ship, it would be safe to assume that the town and kingdom of Bakla were located somewhere on the lower Meghna river, or one of its tributaries, possibly the Tentulia. The *Ain-i-Akbari* of Abul Fazl, the Mughal court officer and chronicler, mentioned some years after Fitch visited the place that the town was destroyed by a giant tidal wave from the sea, taking two hundred thousand lives with it. Bakla reappeared as a Mughal zamindari (estate run by a tax-collecting landlord or zamindar), but on a different and safer location. From old Bakla, Fitch travelled to Sripur and Sonargaon, two midsize kingdoms of the lower Bengal delta, and to Pegu in Burma. Throughout the journey, he carefully noted the tradable goods to be found, from the pepper of Cochin, cloves of the Moluccas, diamonds of Golconda, rubies of Pegu, to the 'great store of Cotton cloth [from Bengal], and much Rice, wherewith they serve all India, Ceilon, Pegu, Malacca, Sumatra, and many other places.' From Pegu, Fitch sailed for England, where he reached on 29 April 1591.

Master Ralph Fitch, one of the minor members of the party, became the most famous among them when the records of the travel appeared in print. Some of the geographical details in the book drew upon the accounts of a Venetian merchant Cesare Fedirici. But this was the first travelogue of India by an Englishman. Fitch became a hero. Ten years after the fleet returned, Shakespeare wrote in *Macbeth*, 'Her husband's to Aleppo gone, master o' the Tyger', making reference to a voyage that evoked immense popular interest in his time. The expedition had not achieved anything to serve trade directly. But it sowed the seeds for the idea that a trade treaty between two kingdoms, Mughal India and Tudor England, could be possible. This objective would be better served some decades later by means of an organized body of merchants, a united Company.

James Lancaster

Three weeks before Fitch's return, London merchants had sponsored the first of three voyages undertaken by one of the most famous merchants and mariners of the time, James Lancaster. The ill-fated expedition saw one of the two main ships go down under a giant wave off the Cape, and the other struck by lightning. The surviving ship did reach the Malacca Straits, thanks to the help received from a Gujarati sailor whom the ship picked up at Zanzibar. The only real success of the expedition occurred in Penang, where it waylaid a Portuguese ship loaded with silk and spice. When returning from Penang, Lancaster's crew had a curious encounter with a sailor who had been left for dead upon the uninhabited St. Helena, and survived a Robinson Crusoe existence for more than a year. Shortly after being picked up he died, allegedly of excessive joy at having met Englishmen. Before he died, he made a most opportune gift of forty goats to the badly provisioned ship. Lancaster then went to the West Indies, lost his ship off the coast of Brazil, and eventually returned empty-handed in a French vessel in 1594. The trip ended in financial failure, but the upside was that the naval engagement in Penang revealed the vulnerability of Portuguese power in the eastern waters.

Lancaster proved his worth as a ship captain, an explorer of great courage, and as the only sailor equally knowledgeable about both the Atlantic and the Indian Ocean highways. Born in England, Lancaster was raised among the Portuguese and spoke the language well, which made him especially suitable to lead the expedition that was to set off the very next month to Brazil in the hope of causing trouble to the Portuguese. The party met this aim to some extent, but not before losing one of its ablest commanders. These setbacks delayed the planning of the next trip to the east, and underscored the need for organizational skills to deal with the Portuguese.

In 1599, the City's moneyed men were again ready to sponsor a trip.

Founders' Hall

On 24 September 1599, an assembly of burghers, mariners, soldiers and notables gathered in the Founders' Hall in the City of London to discuss finances and logistics for another trip. The mariners, among whom were present Lancaster, Fitch, John Davis, Henry Middleton and members of Cavendish and Drake's fleets, persuaded the more circumspect merchants to subscribe capital. Of the burghers, Richard Staper, instrumental in the formation of the Levant Company, and Fitch's companion Eldred, were already converts to the cause. Given these crossovers, it would not be wrong to say that in a sense the company formed with the objective of exploring the Indian Ocean was the Levant Company in a new form. What the mariners had to tell their audience was not only what profits awaited them in spices, but also how few and poorly defended the Portuguese trading stations in the east were. In the next few days, the amount of money raised exceeded £70,000, an impressive sum. Directors were elected, and divided into two committees, one to oversee the shipping, and the other to negotiate with the Crown the royal license to trade.

A petition signed by 215 individuals was submitted to the Queen for the inauguration of the new company. Their commission was not going to be an easy one. Although the Queen was in favour of the enterprise, the pro-Catholic lobby inside the Parliament was against a move that was seen as a potential source of conflict with the Spanish Crown. One of the more interesting outcomes of the ideological clash was the preparation of a fact-finding report based on all documentary and oral evidence available then, on India and Southeast Asia. At the end of a somewhat chaotic list of kingdoms, chiefs, and places, beginning with Diu and ending with Manila, the report concluded, 'In all these, and infinite places more, abounding with greate welth and riches, the Portugals and Spaniards have not any castle, forte, blockhouse, or comaundment, as wee are able to prove'.

The report clinched the issue. On the last day of 1600, the Queen delivered a charter to the merchants, when preparations for the first voyage was already under way. The company, until then provisionally called the Society of Adventurers to the East Indies, started business under the name, The Company of the Merchants of London Trading to the East Indies.

What did a royal charter mean? It created a corporate body legally entitled to own property in its name anywhere in the authorized areas of operation, and entitled to frame its own organizational rules. The Company held exclusive license to trade in the realms of operation, and was authorized to sub-contract the license. In effect, the traders on behalf of the Company were the apprentices, sons and 'factors' hired by the shareholding members of the governing board. The Company was authorized to carry bullion out of the country. On its part of the bargain, it was expected to bring back at least as much bullion as it carried out. The precise sharing of the trading profits between the Queen and the Company was not clearly stated. Any confiscated goods, however, were to be shared 50-50 between them. The charter was to be periodically reviewed. The authorized realm was a huge chunk of the globe, spanned by the Cape of Good Hope at one end and the Strait of Magellan at another, separated by 10,000 miles of open sea by the shortest route.

Not all mariners and merchants had been party to the Founders' Hall group. One such, Edward Michelbourne, had influence in the Court and was offered as a candidate for command of the enterprise. Sensing an impending division, the City merchants stood firm and insisted that 'men of their own qualitye', rather than 'gentlemen' of the court, would suit the enterprise better. Eventually, their perseverance won. But Michelbourne was too influential to be ignored, as we shall see.

Red Dragon

Lancaster, bestowed with the imposing title governor and general, was to lead the first trading mission under the flag of the Company. The first voyage had five ships in all. The largest was Red Dragon, 600 tons with a crew of 202 men and commanded by Lancaster. The other four were Hector, Ascension, Susan and a ship carrying food. Susan was the very first ship purchased by the Company. Excepting Red Dragon, the ships weighed between 240 and 300 tons, and had about 300 persons in all. The main vessel was a sturdy ship, heavily armed, but perhaps too large for the tropical waters by contemporary standards.

What merchandise and supplies did these ships carry? On the assumption of twenty months at sea, the food loaded was worth £6600. What was termed 'investment', were in fact articles of gifts for foreign kings, and cost £4500. These goods consisted of iron, tin, broadcloth and other sundry textiles. The major items of expenditure, however, were bullion to conduct trade, and occasionally make presents, and the salary bill of the sailors. The Queen's charter specified that £30,000 worth of bullion could be carried in the first four voyages of the Company.

In these early ventures, profits were too difficult to estimate, and the payment to the crew was allowed a degree of flexibility. The 'bill of adventure' was a sum of money paid as commission on profits. For example, £500 was to be paid to the pilot-major John Davis of Sandridge, possibly the most famous navigator of his time, if the voyage made 100 per cent profit, double that amount if it made 200 per cent, and so on. In addition to his fixed salary of £100, Davis had access to an allowance of £200 for trade on his own account. No clear rules were made upon the means to earn a profit. The border line between piracy and commerce was indeed very fine. Every sailor was in principle available for battle. Although needless provocation was to be avoided, the sailors had no qualms about raiding a poorly defended solitary ship. Besides mariners and sailors-cum-soldiers, the ships carried 'factors', merchants carrying a sum of money advanced by the Company to trade only on the Company's account. As an incentive, they were also allowed a sum of money as 'adventure', or private trade. The word adventure literally meant private enterprise of uncertain prospects.

On a February morning of 1601, the first voyage set off from the docks at Woolwich. When it reached the Cape, after a reasonably peaceful journey, the crew was devastated by scurvy, and not enough hands were available to run five ships. Hobbling along to the Indian Ocean with four ships, the expedition faced better sailing conditions. But the prospect of trade was still far away.

From the Cape, Lancaster headed straight for Aceh in Sumatra in search of pepper. The kingdoms of the pepper-growing islands already did business with the Europeans. But Englishmen there were none yet in this world. The Sultan of Aceh received Lancaster with a warm welcome. Giant elephants carried him and his companions to the palace, to join a banquet complete with beautiful bejeweled dancing girls. All very well, but where was the pepper? The English found little in the market, being sold at far higher prices than they had expected to pay, and much of it already booked by the Portuguese and the Dutch. One option was to establish a trading station in the country, which would have the time to accumulate supplies steadily. Such a post would need to be defended against the European rivals. But a Portuguese proposal of a fortified trading station had already been indignantly dismissed by the king. There was, however, another solution to the dilemma.

Lancaster, who had struck a cordial note with the king, sought permission to target-practice on the Portuguese. The king agreed, on condition that Lancaster would obtain for him a Portuguese girl after the battle. Within a few days, a Portuguese ship, unusually large at 900 tons in weight and filled with pepper and clove, was waylaid, bombarded and captured by the English. In one morning's work, Lancaster had made his fortune, and made the voyage pay its capital many times over. The business of taking leave of the king finished with fanfare and goodwill. Sadly for the king, in this rough world of sailors and soldiers, no European girl had been found worthy of him. Lancaster headed now towards the Sunda Straits for Bantam in Western Java, and did obtain trading privileges from the Sultan of Bantam. Like many such promises made in this time, it meant little unless backed up by the constant presence of an armed fleet. The journey back to England almost ended in tragedy when the ships met with a cyclone off the Cape. Lancaster dismissed all suggestions of abandoning his badly damaged ship, and braved the wind.

The party returned in September 1603, to find that

the Queen had died in their absence. The pepper alone that the fleet had brought back was valued at more than a million pounds. The other goods added a mighty sum to the total. Lancaster returned a hero and the Company had as glorious a start as any merchant firm of the time could hope for.

Within a few months of the first voyage, the rival Michelbourne had pulled strings to have a voyage to China and Japan sanctioned by the court. The expedition was an ill-fated one. He had a brush with the Dutch and a series of violent skirmishes with the Japanese that saw his best crew, including Davis, die in battle. But he had set a trend, that of defying the Company's charter of exclusive rights in the eastern waters. He had gone down in the history books as the first 'interloper'.

A new business model

Fifteen more expeditions set out for pepper in the next fifteen years. The enterprise of making voyages settled down to a stable and predictable pattern. The risks were reduced. Knowledge of trading opportunities increased, and trade rather than raid became the goal of these journeys. In the beginning the Company bought the ships that it needed. But the risk of damage or loss was so high that the risk-covered prices of ships became unaffordable, and the Company began building ships in Deptford, a shipyard leased in for the purpose. With the knowledge that the ill fortunes of some of the voyages had owed to the small size of the ships, much larger ones were built. The very largest ship in a long time to come, the prosaic Trade's Increase of 1000 tons, was built in 1609. The move did bring down the costs of ships per ton of cargo, but added much overhead costs to the operation. In the 1630s, the Company got rid of Deptford and started hiring ships, some of them continued to be built in the same shipyards under private ownership.

The pool of expert seamen from which the commanders could be recruited was larger than before. Unlike an earlier generation, for whom the potential gains from these voyages had been unknown, those who joined as crew in the 1610s saw the prospect of profits more clearly. There was steadily increasing enlistment into the crew. More of them tended to be proficient in Spanish, Dutch, Arabic and Portuguese, the languages of the sea. The older Atlantic merchant marine was the 'nursery' that supplied the Indian Ocean commanders of this generation. Some of the first generation voyagers, especially Lancaster, had joined the Company as directors, and their leadership enabled the Company to organize trips with more precise economic aims rather than the opportunistic missions of an earlier era. The ships now had chaplains, surgeons, musical instruments, facilities for staging Shakespearian plays and a more disciplined crew. Above all, the whole enterprise was exceedingly profitable. The distributed profit on the first voyage was 300 per cent. Distributed profits in all of the East India voyages together exceeded 200 per cent every year until 1616.

Nevertheless, the first fifteen years were not smooth sailing. True, the internal constitution remained intact; the first governor, Thomas Smith, merchant and alderman, remained in office until 1621; and the Company succeeded in sending one expedition every year as specified in the charter. But it had to battle with three adversities. The first problem was capital. The business of spice carried risks. One bad expedition could bankrupt the Company. Fearing for their money, many of the Company's shareholders did not fully pay up their capital, adopting a wait-and-watch policy on the current voyage. The Company had to go around with a begging bowl after every voyage in order to finance the next one. A second problem arose from fluctuations in demand for luxuries. There were not too many buyers available for the eastern spices at the prevailing exorbitant rates. When a few of them died in a plague epidemic, stocks built up to disastrous levels.

The third problem arose from what was known as the separate voyages system. Partly on account of the precarious finances, the shareholders divided into groups, and the lobbies and clubs among them individually funded voyages. The practice divided loyalty, for these financiers expected to have the first call upon the profits from a voyage that they had paid more money for. Apart from compromising the economic interests represented by the firm, the separate voyages weakened diplomatic efforts, which had to be undertaken by common consent and for a common purpose, and left the military enterprise to the temperaments of individual commanders of fleets. These features imparted a dangerous informality to the whole enterprise.

Hoping to settle all these problems at once, the Company declared itself a joint-stock concern in 1612. The prodigious sum of £429,000 was raised as capital. The threat of bankruptcy was substantially reduced. Orders henceforth were issued only in the names of the high officials, governor and deputy governor. Above all, it placed the political aspect of the business upon a firmer footing.

If these measures settled problems at home, the trading enterprise was beginning to run into a formidable obstacle overseas. Nearly all of the early voyages were induced by the lure of spices from Southeast Asia. In the Southeast Asian trade, the Portuguese challenge was primarily naval, and could be overcome with military means. But the Dutch, who were already entrenched in trade and were a more organized enemy, proved more difficult to handle.

The Dutch East India Company had followed the English one by two years. It was a slightly different entity from the English Company. It was initially a shipping cartel. Ship-owning merchants decided to pool capital, and form a unified management, partly because they felt threatened by similar moves made by their English counterparts. Company formation occurred in the Dutch republic in a somewhat different way from the process in England. The power of the royalty was relatively weak after the Dutch Provinces joined together; consequently, major mercantile decisions took place independent of the court. Between 1595 and 1599, merchants of Amsterdam and Rotterdam had fitted every ship they could lay their hands on and sent these off in search of spices. Unlike the English who travelled along the Cape route made dangerous by the Portuguese, some of the Dutch ships took the safer but longer route via the Strait of Magellan to reach South Pacific. The Company found it hard to engage with and overcome Dutch resistance in the western Pacific. It began, therefore, to think of a more indirect strategy of procuring the spices.

All the rival Western European powers trying to procure Indonesian spices understood the critical role of India in making the spice trade possible. The commodity that sold best in Southeast Asia was Indian cotton cloth. Further, spice-laden ships needed to call in at Indian ports to restock food and repair ships. It was, therefore, essential to establish a partnership between India and the trading stations further east. For the English, Bantam needed a partner in India. Surat was the obvious choice for its strategic location and existing reputation as the leading entrepôt in the subcontinent. The difficulty was that Surat was firmly a part of the Mughal empire.

MISSION TO INDIA

FROM THE VERY inception of the Company, the directors understood the strategic need to establish contact with what they called the Court of the Grand Mogul. Trade and its protection against all adversaries were essential to the success of the whole enterprise and this could not be ensured only by armed engagement. The Dutch, the early comers, adopted mainly military means, with a dose of judicious bribing, to establish a foothold in India. The English began in the same fashion, but went further than the Dutch in establishing diplomatic relations with Indian rulers.

John Mildenhall and William Hawkins

A year before the Company was incorporated, a mission sponsored by the court and headed by a merchant, John

Mildenhall, came to Agra. Mildenhall travelled over land, arriving there in 1603. He was courteously received, and was offered a formal but useless license to trade. The Portuguese and the Jesuits in Akbar's court conspired to scuttle his mission. In the bargain, Mildenhall learnt Persian, and when he returned to England in 1608, was appointed by the Levant Company to represent them in Persia. His last years ended in controversy. For some time, the Company lost contact with him and suspected him to be a Persian spy. During this time, he married a Persian woman and had two children by her. The Company agents caught up with him again in Punjab. He died in Ajmer, declaring a Frenchman, from whom he had extracted a promise to marry his daughter, the executor of his estate. The prospective son-in-law promptly burned all of Mildenhall's account books, destroying any evidence that could redeem his reputation or otherwise.

In August 1608 a fleet commanded by the merchant and sea captain William Hawkins, possibly the same Hawkins who as a boy had accompanied Drake in 1577 to the Atlantic, reached Surat, hoping to make contact with the Mughal governor. The Portuguese tried to stop him, even though England and Portugal were at that moment at peace. When Hawkins finally managed to establish links with the governor Makarrab Khan, much of his resources were dissipated in making gifts, without any serious purpose being achieved. Since the governor's writ did not run very far from the borders of the town, Hawkins took the desperate decision to travel to Agra over land. He gathered a retinue of Pathan horsemen, dressed up as an Afghan nobleman, and reached Agra in 1609.

Unknown to the party, Emperor Jahangir had kept himself informed of its progress. An audience was quickly arranged, and was immediately successful. The emperor listened patiently to a translation of the letter from the English king James I, received the mandatory assortment of gifts, commented on his guest's good looks, and was delighted to find that they shared a knowledge of Arabic, in which they conversed from then on. The English were issued a license to build a factory at Surat. So eager was Jahangir to display his affection for his new found friend that he was not satisfied with granting him a mere license. He conferred on Hawkins the title of 400-horse mansabdar (an entitlement to command soldiers), and found for him an Armenian girl to marry.

Hawkins' letters to his superiors during his stay in Agra painted the picture of an alcoholic despot suffering from violent mood swings. Whether Jahangir came to know about these missives or Makarrab Khan and the

Portuguese poisoned his mind, he tired of Hawkins as quickly as he had grown fond of him. Although an English factory in name continued in Surat, Hawkins himself had to leave in 1611 on a ship bound for Bantam.

Another Company mission to India happened by accident. The real objective of this expedition, the sixth fleet sent out by the Company, was to establish trading rights and a foothold in Aden, then under the charge of a governor of the Ottomans. The mission ended in a battle, and the commander Henry Middleton found himself a hostage of the Aga. Upon his escape, he recovered near Dabhol and Surat, to the annoyance of the Portuguese. His stay on the coast, however, did not lead to anything further, for Middleton was bent upon revenge and returned to Aden. Disagreements in his ranks saw these moves fail too. Not one to give up, he made a trip to Bantam to pick up Hawkins to join hands with him. Unfortunately, Hawkins died on the voyage of an epidemic disease that swept through the ship. Middleton died in 1611 in the knowledge of a mission blighted by ill luck and bad judgement.

As for Hawkins's widow, she returned to England, remarried a mariner, possibly the famous Gabriel Towerson who was executed by the Dutch in Amboyna in 1623, and was last seen in Surat haranguing the English for a suitable pension.

Thomas Best and Nicholas Downton

Two further voyages to Surat were hardly more consequential in meeting the main aims of the English. Thomas Best, a forty-year-old sea captain with experience of commanding ships to Russia and the Levant, was appointed head of the tenth fleet in December 1611. Three weeks after anchoring at Surat, Best was attacked by a strong Portuguese force. The two battles that ensued saw Best score a complete victory, and earned him the Mughal emperor's permission to allow the English right to trade.

On the second occasion, Nicholas Downton, who had earlier commanded the disastrous sixth fleet, was chosen to command a voyage in 1614, which went to Surat to secure a trading operation there. A fleet led by the viceroy of Goa, Jeronimo de Azevedo, arrived to drive out the English. The English were vastly outnumbered, but proved to be better gunners. Having lost 500 of his men, whereas the English lost only five, Don Jeronimo gave up the fight and returned to Goa. This battle more or less marked the end of Portuguese power on the western seaboard. The relationship between the Mughal agents and the Portuguese had already soured, and the outcome of these battles, keenly followed from the shore, was welcomed by the former. Downton received the now customary letter from Agra promising unrestricted freedom to trade. His own health, however, had suffered and he died soon after in Bantam.

By 1612, a small band of English traders were manning an English trading outpost in Surat. Thomas Kerridge, the first chief of the outpost, stated in his reports that sword-blades, knives, broadcloth, lead and quicksilver found a ready market in Surat. In turn he was buying indigo, medicinal substances, cotton yarn, especially calico, the plain white cotton cloth that found ready market in Southeast Asia. Kerridge instructed his principals to send English bulldogs, which made an excellent gift for the Indian kings. Earlier, in 1609 or 1610, one Mr Aldworth of the factory journeyed by road to Ahmedabad, passing on his way Boroatch (Bharuch) and Bothra (Vadodara). He had reported that excellent and cheap calicoes and indigo were to be found in these interior towns, but that in order to procure these goods on a sustained basis it would be necessary to have a permanent diplomatic mission stationed in Agra, a lot of ready cash, and a strong military backing.

The Surat team knew that a mere imperial edict did not mean very much in practical terms. On each occasion when the English fleet had left Surat, those who remained behind were obstructed by numerous local orders, to be lifted only on payment of money to the governor and his courtiers. What Best and Downton did achieve was a reputation in the Mughal court for English mastery over the seas, which to the Mughals was very critical as they did not have a navy of their own. With this reputation behind them, the Company shifted its diplomatic tactics and sought to establish a direct link between the English monarchy and the Mughal emperor, which would then give it the legitimacy to deal with the Mughal court as equals. But their experiences had also shown that setting up a viable trade mission in India was beyond the capability of mariners. The job needed a seasoned diplomat. It fell upon Thomas Roe to carry it out.

Thomas Roe

Roe (1581–1644) came from a landowning family of Essex. Having completed his matriculation in Oxford (at the age of twelve!), Roe spent the next five years as a student in the Middle Temple, a finishing school for future court officers, and joined court service at age twenty. He rose quickly in position, and was entrusted with several daring as well as delicate tasks, including an expedition to seek the fabled El Dorado, the gold-laden city lost in the forests of the Andes, and sorting out Princess Elizabeth's dire finances. His reputation as a courageous and honest officer stayed with him throughout. When in October 1614 the king invited Roe to go to India as ambassador, he did not hesitate in accepting a job that was going to be no less difficult than looking for El Dorado.

Roe's mission took full four years to come to a conclusion. During these years, Roe followed the camp of Jahangir from Ajmer to Mandu, falling in and out and back in favour with the emperor. These swings partly depended on the quality of the presents made to the emperor. English mastiffs, Irish greyhounds and red wine delighted him. In a match arranged in an enclosed courtyard, the mastiffs attacked an elephant so fiercely that the highly impressed monarch appointed a team of servants to feed them with silver spoons and fan the flies away from them. But many of the routine presents like cloths, pictures and boxes, which the English considered worthy of a king, bored him. Roe's mission was made difficult by the switching sympathies of Prince Khurram (later Shah Jahan) from the English to the Portuguese. The prime minister Asaf Khan was also in two minds over granting special favours to the English. Communication was another serious impediment to worthwhile dialogue with the Mughals. Roe communicated with the courtiers in a very indirect fashion through a Portuguese Jesuit priest who translated his Latin into Persian. Neither language was native to the speakers. All along, the Dutch, who had already been settled in the eastern port Masulipatnam, tried to frustrate the English efforts at diplomacy.

If Roe succeeded, it was primarily because he was different from his predecessors in the imperial court. He was not a merchant-mariner. He was an officer of the king, and his appearance, bearing and education made this amply clear. Through gentle persuasion, firmness in his dealings with Khurram, and a steadily improving equation with Jahangir and Asaf Khan, Roe succeeded in obtaining a license to trade from the emperor.

In theory Roe got nothing more substantial than the usual promises that Best and Downton had received before. Roe's intention, by contrast, was to bring the emperor to a more permanent commitment, and it appears that his strategy to that effect was to make the contract as complete and binding as possible. A detailed and precise set of instructions and clauses added legitimacy to the contract, made the seriousness of purpose more evident to the local British officers, and divided responsibilities for implementation of the contract between the two parties. The document that Roe prepared for Jahangir to sign upon was less than ideal for this purpose, but it was still the first authentic contractual agreement ever drawn up concerning private commerce by a sovereign of India. In the Indian scenario, it was nothing short of a new paradigm. It was a treaty between two sovereigns rather than a one-sided grant of royal favour as the previous orders had been.

Running into the Dutch, again!

By 1610, the Dutch and the English were the powers on the rise in the Indian Ocean. Competition between these two armed rivals threatened to break out in violence on numerous occasions. If they did not after all engage in a fight to the finish, that restraint owed partly to their shared dislike for the Portuguese, and partly from a sense that whoever won a decisive engagement would emerge the absolute master of the seas, and no one wanted to take the risk. They came to blows many times in the seventeenth century, but a debilitating conflict was avoided.

When Roe's mission ended, the Dutch were securely positioned in Java. The Dutch and the English were friends in Europe, but in southeast Asia, Dutch ships intimidated and drove off English ships whenever possible, retaining a substantial control over the spice trade. The two fleets were so evenly matched in power that a proposal to merge the two Companies to form a huge monopoly did not surprise anyone. The proposal came from the Dutch side in 1615, but fell through after the English investigators realized that the Dutch ran their enterprise with massive doses of borrowed money.

The next seven or eight years went by in this curious combination of cautious friendship in Europe and bickering in Southeast Asia. Matters came to a head with the execution of Towerson, an agent of the English Company, along with nine Englishmen and a few Japanese mariners by the Dutch in 1623 for plotting to storm the fort in Amboyna. No more than a case of trade rivalry that went out of control, the episode became known in England as 'the massacre of Amboyna' and evoked a sharp reaction to the treachery of the Dutch. The two parties agreed upon a truce only from shared fear of the Portuguese. But the alliance was far from a happy one. 'All in all,' the Dutch governor-general explained, 'a disagreeable wife is bestowed on us.'

The Persian campaign

In West Asia, on the other hand, a conflict was brewing between the Portuguese and the English over trading rights in the Persian empire. Hormuz was the principal entrepôt on the mouth of the Persian Gulf, where caravan trade met maritime trade. Persia provided valuable silks to Europe. It was also a source for horses, for which there was an insatiable demand among Indian kings. In effect, it was the first item in the trading chain that spanned Persia, India and Indonesia. Horses bought in Persia were traded for cotton in India which in turn was exchanged for spices in Indonesia. The catch in this arrangement was that Hormuz and the Gulf were dominated by the Portuguese.

The English in the Gulf pursued a strategy of diplomacy backed by military power not unlike the one that succeeded in India. Robert Sherley (or Shirley) was initially employed by the British to establish communication with Shah Abbas of Persia. Sherley was a mariner of aristocratic antecedents who had settled in the Persian capital and married the daughter of a Circassian nobleman. In 1608, he was appointed by the Shah as the ambassador to the court of James I, where he caused a sensation by arriving with his Circassian wife with the regalia and fanfare befitting a Persian courtier. In 1615, he was sent as ambassador to Portugal and Spain. The precise purpose of these missions is not known, and how well Sherley met the aims cannot be adjudged. In any case, when he returned to Persia in 1620, he was summarily dismissed from Persian royal service and died soon after. His role in facilitating the interests of the Company in Persia though not insignificant, was indirect at best.

It was Edward Connock, an appointee of the Company, who achieved in Persia what Roe had achieved in India two years earlier, the grant of a royal license. Connock was well-received in the court, the treaty was celebrated with copious amounts of wine, and in this merry atmosphere the Shah made a deal with Connock to supply 3000 bales of silk annually to England at an agreed price. Some of this bonhomie owed to the Shah's hope of forming a joint front to oust the Portuguese from the Gulf. The moment of reckoning came in December 1620. A Surat fleet under Andrew Shilling encountered a fleet sent from Lisbon led by Ruy Freire de Andrade. In the bloody engagements that followed, the English commander died and honours were almost equally shared, but Freire de Andrade surrendered. Hormuz fell in April 1621. Thereafter, the Company could envisage its commercial operations in terms of Hormuz (horses for cloth), Surat (cloth for spices), and Bantam (spices) together. In this three-cornered system, the Company's interests in Southeast Asia prevailed over those in India, but the India trade was growing at the same time.

Until about 1640, all of the Company's operations in India were placed under the administration of Surat. The relationship with the Mughal authorities was stable, if not one of warm friendship. Much was achieved towards securing the Company's position on the west coast of India by two individuals, William Methwold and John Weddell. Methwold, the first 'president' of Surat, arrived on the western coast when the region had been devastated by a famine and piracy. A little before his arrival, the Company ships had established contacts with the Zamorin, the ruler of Calicut, to enable them to purchase spices from Kerala, and conduct joint missions to harass the Portuguese in Goa. But these moves exposed them to attacks by Malabar pirates. Not very successful in curbing piracy, Methwold was more successful in negotiating peace with the Portuguese. He was also the first influential officer to broach the idea of creating a harbour in Bombay. Methwold returned to England to become a full-time director of the Company. John Weddell helped in making the Surat-Persia connection stronger. He was a sea captain, a hero of the battle of Hormuz, and had been sent on a number of trading-cum-naval missions by the Company in the early 1630s before he was indicted for private trade.

From the 1640s, this three-cornered system began to fail. Too many Englishmen died in Persia from disease. And Dutch machinations weakened the English position further. On the death of William Gibson, the agent in Isfahan, examination of his account books revealed that Gibson was trading on his own in collaboration with the Dutch merchants. Treachery had joined with interloping. In interior Persia, Armenian merchants reigned supreme, and who ruled the seaboard depended on who were friendlier with the Armenians. On this point too, the Dutch proved smarter. Lastly, the English Civil War (1642–51) reduced the market for a luxury item like silk, the chief article of merchandise from Persia. The decline of Persia as a factor in the three-cornered trade meant that the English needed to find other means of payments for Indian textiles than horses. Silver was to grow in importance as the principal means of payment.

A House divided

Weddell's infamy as a private trader symbolized a growing problem. From very early on, the Company had had to deal with resourceful individuals who defied its monopoly. In the first thirty years, the problem had grown, as Company employees who completed their periods of indenture and did not return to England, routinely took part in private trade. Other merchants, called voluntaries, paid money to the court to buy the right to trade in the eastern waters. A cash-strapped Charles I, committed to expensive warfare at home and abroad, was ready to grant such privileges for a consideration.

Realizing that there was little that it could do to suppress and punish so many rebels, the Company settled on a compromise. It allowed private business except in a few goods reserved for exclusive trade, on the condition that the traders would take a licence. It was also more tolerant of private transactions between ports within the same territory, as opposed to overseas trade.

In 1635, a leading silk and linen merchant of London, William Courten, along with an influential courtier Endymion Porter, approached the king to obtain a charter for a new East India Company. The mission of the new company was to conduct trade in the Portuguese spheres of influence, Goa, Malabar, China and Japan, establish trading stations in Australia, and start a colony in Madagascar. The new partnership, financed by a leading merchant of the city Paul Pindar, received permission to carry gold and was justified as an enterprise that operated in areas neglected by the old company. The old company was furious at the commission, but could not do anything to stop it. Funded by a massive investment of £120,000, the first voyage of the new company set out under the captaincy of John Weddell.

This voyage included Peter Mundy, whose account of the expedition remains an important source on Weddell and the regions that he went to. The first expedition went to a number of places, the most important of which was Canton. It was a mixed success, which Courten did not live to see. Pirate raids and shipwrecks led to huge loss of cargo. Yet, what was brought home was sufficient to alarm the directors of the old company. The first voyage was also significant for being one of the first English visits to coastal China. When returning from the next voyage to Goa and Masulipatnam, Weddell mysteriously disappeared. An 'eyewitness' stated that he had been invited to a Dutch ship, and after being entertained there, was thrown overboard. The Dutch might have wanted to do this to him, but the more likely explanation of the disappearance was a shipwreck off the Cape of Good Hope in the winter of 1639.

The story of the new company was disastrous from this point onward. Saddled with inherited debt, the second son of Courten, also called William, continued his father's mission. But the son's personal fortunes plummeted despite sympathetic assistance from the king. The old company left nothing undone to obstruct the new company's enterprise. He petitioned the Parliament against these actions without success. In 1643, the Dutch captured some of his ships off the Straits of Malacca. Courten fled from his creditors to Italy, where he died bankrupt in 1655. By then the new company had been merged into the old.

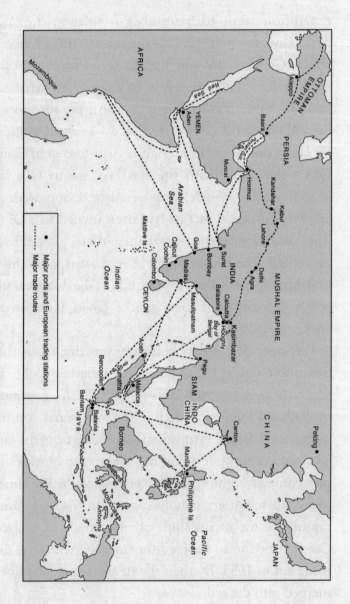

Major maritime and overland trade routes in the Indian Ocean, c. 1700.

MADRAS, BOMBAY AND CALCUTTA

HORMUZ HAD BEEN a dubious prize from a trading point of view. Already in decline, English victory over the Portuguese more or less sealed its fate. On the other hand, the conquest of Hormuz escalated hostility in the Konkan. In 1626, after several years of uneasy truce, the Dutch and the English conducted a joint operation to raid Bassein, located on 'the Bay of Bumbaye'. A well-situated but almost unused port in Portuguese possession, Bumbaye contained no more than a poorly defended fort and a settlement of fishermen. The Portuguese command escaped to Goa before the forces arrived, and the invaders had to be happy with a few bags of rice they left behind. The intensity of Anglo-Portuguese conflicts in the Indian waters died down from then onward. A truce was signed between the English and the Portuguese in 1634, ushering in an unusually long-lasting peace.

As a result of these conflicts, the Company's officers had already started discussing among themselves the need to build forts in their trading stations. The idea was not a new one. The Portuguese had shown the way. Although the Indian Ocean ceased to be a battleground in the 1630s, the Dutch maintained a larger military presence than the English. The death of Shah Jahan and the wars of succession in the 1660s added further to the growing feeling of insecurity. Between 1632 and 1690, three fortified settlements came up in India, in Madras, Bombay and Calcutta, in that order. These three sites embodied a whole new package of trade, naval defence, and politics, which would become the focal point of Company trade and territorial expansion in the eighteenth century.

Madras

The Company's seventh voyage of 1611 under Anthony Hippon had attempted to set up a factory on the Coromandel at Pulicat, in the hope of sharing the coast-to-coast trade with the Dutch who were already stationed there. The move failed due to Dutch protestation in the court of the queen who ruled that part of the coast. Hippon then sailed north towards the mouth of the river Krishna. Although a coast well known for cyclonic storms, the spot where he chose to land was reasonably sheltered from the sea. Nothing further came of this trip, even though a settlement of some sort continued here until 1687, when, repeatedly ravaged by fevers, it was dismantled. Three years after Hippon, another expedition to Pulicat was thwarted. After hosting the English to a lavish banquet, the Dutch forbade them to trade.

Hippon and his companions carried on and landed at Masulipatnam where a more permanent but small station was set up. This port was ruled by the agents of Golconda, who wanted it to become a free port rather than a monopoly of any single European power. It was not until 1632 that Golconda's own authority over Masulipatnam was secure enough for the English to trade freely. For some time, therefore, the English also tried a 'miserable' shelter called Armagaon. When they returned to Masulipatnam in 1632, they found that the weavers and dyers who had earlier supplied them cloth had all died in the 1630 famine.

Nevertheless, the importance of Coromandel grew as a partner in trade with Bantam. Coromandel supplied the cotton cloth used as payment for pepper.

Coromandel, in addition, was the source of hand-painted cotton in great demand in Europe and Asia alike. Another big attraction of Coromandel was the trade in diamonds from Golconda, which formed both a lucrative commodity as also a means of remitting money from India to Europe.

In 1632, Francis Day (1605–70) arrived in the nearly ruined factory at Armagaon as a Company factor. Surrounded by hostile powers, Day began to look for a safer place for a factory. On a journey from Masulipatnam to Pondicherry, he settled on a spot between two villages, Madrasipatnam and Chinnapatnam. Located close to a Portuguese church and settlement, the site was purchased from the local ruler Damarla Venkatadri. Day described many advantages of the site to his colleagues at Masulipatnam. Cloth was cheaper to obtain, the coast was good for landing, the settlement was nearer the sources of painted cloth, and above all, the friendly local ruler had offered to construct the fort there before Day moved in, on the promise that he would be reimbursed in the form of Persian horses.

When Day arrived in 1640, he discovered to his horror that the king had in mind a fort made of palmyra leaves. Taking matters into his own hands, he began constructing a fort with sturdier raw materials, possibly on St George's Day. The move did not make London happy, so Day had to start construction with his own money. The powers in London left any decision to prevent the coming up of the fort or punishment of Day to the Surat authorities. Officials in Surat, in turn, 'hoped' that the factors in Coromandel had considered all possible angles before building a fort there. In this way, the Fort St George in Madras became possible because Surat and Masulipatnam joined Day in quietly ignoring the Company headquarters in London.

What saved the settlement from a damaging disciplinary action was its immediate success as a commercial centre. Within months, dozens of weavers' families came to Madras and started living there. Families of merchants and artisans residing in the Portuguese colony San Thome shifted residence to the English area. Although the Portuguese grudgingly accepted the English fort, and the Dutch watched in alarm from Pulicat, neither of them chose to act. Madras did not fail to supply sufficient cloth to Bantam. A French Capuchin monk, Father Ephraim de Nevers, built a place of worship for the spiritual benefit of Catholics and others alike. And, what might surprise the present-day visitor to the city, a Spanish traveller in the 1630s described the climate of Madras as 'excellent'.

Day was summoned to England for punitive action in

the summer of 1841. At the end of an enquiry he was sent back with a bundle of letters authorizing the decision. However, as a face saver for the Company, he and other decision-makers were chastised for needless extravagance. In 1642, the head office of the Coromandel operations shifted from Masulipatnam to Madras. For this decision, Day received the support of the agent of Masulipatnam, Andrew Cogan. The support made a difference, for Cogan was both influential and forceful. In 1657, Fort St George ceased to be subordinate to Bantam, as it had been until then, and was elevated to the position of an independent trading station. Day returned to England in 1645. Not much is known about his life and career after this.

Unlike Surat or Masulipatnam, where the English merely had the right to reside and conduct trade, in the Fort St George they were landlords. It was a precarious title, but nonetheless did make the Company a territorial power on a small scale. In order to hold on to that power without the help of local rulers, the Madras authorities built a wall around the six square miles over which they had proprietary rights and protected it with a garrison. The wall and the garrison were again expenses considered ill-advised by London. The first colonial city in India came up inside these walls. Just outside the walls, a large colony of artisans and service providers came to live. Later designated 'white' and 'black' towns respectively, in the 1670s, these two areas, already sharply demarcated, were described by John Fryer as the Christian Town and the Heathen Town. Thomas Bowrey, a private merchant who left a record of the place in the 1670s, reckoned that the two settlements together had a population of 40,000, which was a good size for a purely commercial town of this time. Many amongst the wealthier Indians of the town were Tamil artisans and Telugu merchants.

European settlements in the Coromandel were periodically exposed to territorial disputes. The Chandragiri kings who had granted the English the title to Madras were caught up in succession wars in the 1640s. Golconda, Bijapur and the Nayakas of Madura, Tanjore and Gingee became embroiled in a struggle for mastery over southern Deccan. The Dutch and the English settlements were alternately protected and threatened by these rivals. In 1646, a new threat materialized from the north, a combined Mughal army under Mir Jumla which defeated the rebellious Nayakas and came within two days' march from Madras. Mir Jumla returned after confirming the English right to continue trading. The fact that his own army depended heavily on European gunners and generals may have played a part in this decision. More important to the

survival of the Europeans settlements was the strength
of their own military power, which could withstand
attacks by the armies that the local states were able to
put up.

A difficult problem was raised when the shadow of
English politics fell on Madras in 1665. Edward Winter,
one of the more capable of the Company's local officers,
was the president of Fort St George then. Winter's plans
to build up the navy and pose an effective deterrent to
the Dutch alarmed the directors at home, who sent the
cautious George Foxcroft to replace him. Foxcroft
arrived in Madras with his son Nathaniel to a frosty
reception from Winter and his retinue. The ensuing
dispute between the two factions carried shades of a
conflict between the royalists, to which camp Winter
belonged, and the 'levellers', which Nathaniel revealed
himself to be. A mutiny broke out, and the Foxcrofts
were thrown in prison. For the next three years, Winter
reigned in Madras despite warnings from the Company
bosses in London, and stepped aside only when the
Company sent a fleet in 1668. To a royal commission of
enquiry, the whole affair was more complicated than
insubordination. The Winter faction claimed to be
working for the Crown in using the Company's
resources to defend Madras. And yet, it had defied the
orders of its employer. In 1672, when the two

protagonists, Winter and Foxcroft senior sailed for England, the matter was closed. But Winter received no punishment for causing the dispute.

Bombay

In 1661, the Anglo-Portuguese peace efforts secured its supreme success, in the marriage between Charles II and the Infanta Catherine. The diplomatic missions discussed a number of matrimonial deals and concluded one. The processing leading to it had much to do with the insecurity in south Asia. The Portuguese felt more threatened by the Dutch, who had shown no intention of following the English in ending hostilities. In 1656, Ceylon, where Portuguese settlement and rule had lasted 170 years, was lost to the Dutch. Could Goa be far behind? On their part, the Company was acutely aware that, with or without Mughal licenses, its position in Surat, and the east coast settlements of Balasore and Hooghly, was precariously dependent on local kings. A new well defended factory away from the Indian territories was the only solution. A factory did come up in Rajapur in Konkan, then in the sphere of influence of the Siddis, but it was never seriously in contention to become the centre of activity. Bombay, on the other hand, because of its natural advantages of a good bay and harbour had many backers within the council in Surat. Charles II led the way to acquiring Bombay, by accepting it as dowry for his bride Catherine of Braganza from the Portuguese Crown. The king gifted it in turn to the Company seven years later. The important consequence of rising English power in the Konkan, therefore, was the acquisition of a new port.

The transfer of Bombay to the Company did not have any immediate impact. Taking possession of the island was a challenge because the Portuguese settlement in Bombay resisted the English, and the royalists resisted the Company's representatives. The locally settled Portuguese communities already possessed a system of governance, including land tenure and taxation. They opposed British occupation from the fear that these interests would be lost. Bombay's coastal waters were unsafe for the English due to pirate attacks from bases in Malabar and Diu, both beyond the reach of the English. The Dutch were upset with the transaction because they wanted Bombay for themselves, and so were the Mughal authorities who claimed a tenuous property right in the area. Neither possessed sufficient military power to force the issue. But the threat of an invasion was never far away.

Complicating matters further, there materialized the prospect of a move upon Bombay by Shivaji's army. A state of war then existed in the Deccan between the Mughals and Shivaji. Surat, being a Mughal city, was exposed to raids by Shivaji's forces. The richest merchants of both Bombay and Surat were employed by the Company or worked under its protection, and they felt deeply insecure. In the course of the ensuing skirmishes, a few Englishmen had in fact been imprisoned by the Marathas.

In a large measure, it was the leadership of two able visionaries—Geoge Oxenden (1620–69) and Gerald Aungier (1635–77)—that saw the Company through these difficulties. Oxenden hailed from a wealthy family of Kent and came to India in 1632 at the age of twelve as an attendant to a priest. His fluency in Hindustani was quickly noticed, and he was offered a job of part-time interpreter in Surat and Ahmedabad. In 1641, he joined as a factor in Surat at a small salary. The greater part of the next twenty years was spent in India on trading missions and constant negotiations with the local rulers and rival companies. His commercial success and political experience made him suitable for the most important job in India, president in Surat, in 1661.

The first two years of his tenure were devoted to settling the problems of Bombay. In January 1664, he faced the most important military challenge of his career, protecting Surat's interests from Shivaji's army. The Company's warehouse was one of the main targets of the Maratha raid, which intended to raise funds for war rather than conquer the city. The Company's employees and traders fought a determined battle and managed to save the property. The defence was led by Oxenden and conducted by civilians. After it ended, the episode brought the Mughal governor and the Company even closer with a marked role reversal—for the first time in the Company's history the Mughals were dependent on the English. In the last years of his office, Oxenden oversaw the end of the royalist-versus-Company dispute over the possession of Bombay by means of letters of patent granting the Company full authority over the island (1668). Oxenden died in Surat the following year.

Aungier came from a family of Irish clergy, and joined the Company's service in 1661 at the age of twenty-six. He too was a factor in Surat, and worked in this capacity for the next seven years. He rose quickly to the second most important position in the Surat council, owing to a deep understanding of the geopolitics of the western coast. On the death of Oxenden in 1669, he succeeded him as president in Surat and as the governor of Bombay. He laid the initial foundations of a form of European government in India. He set up courts, made laws, built a town administration that had representation of the major communities and installed a land tenure and taxation system. The first town plan, land reclamation and fortifications were started. Aungier urged his superiors to relocate the centre of the Company's activities in India from Surat to Bombay. The wisdom of this move was recognized in 1684, seven years after Aungier died in Surat.

At the time of Aungier's death, the charge of the Company's fleet and army was with Richard Keigwin, a sea captain who had distinguished himself in the defence of St Helena during the Anglo-Dutch Wars of 1672. Bombay continued to be a potential target of a Maratha attack and the buildup of a Maratha navy had been a source of worry to the English settlement for some time. Keigwin favoured armed defensive action rather than negotiating with the Marathas. When the Maratha attack did occur in October 1679, Keigwin was well prepared, and he successfully defended Bombay. However, already before this battle, the Company had issued an order to have him removed as commandant, alarmed at the military expenditure that he was incurring. Keigwin defended his case so well that two years later he was back with the rank of captain-lieutenant. There followed another curious period of struggle over expenses, which ended with Keigwin declaring Bombay a Crown territory of which he was the head.

Not surprisingly, he received wide popular support

from within the town's population. Two issues were working in favour of the group that the Company called 'mutineers'. One was the fear of Maratha invasion. Another was the enthusiastic support of interlopers. Thanks to this combination, the administration of Bombay continued in the hands of the mutineers until 1684. In that year the new head of Surat, John Child, arrived off Bombay and started a peace settlement. Child received half-hearted support from London. When Keigwin finally decided to quit and go back to England, he won a royal pardon and was appointed captain of a frigate bound for the West Indies.

Calcutta

Full fifty years after Ralph Fitch had set foot there the Company set its sights upon Bengal. Bengal had many advantages for the kind of business the Company did. Its cotton cloth came in huge variety and low prices. Bengal was well served with rivers, which were convenient for moving cargo. The region already had established trade contact with Arakan, Burma and Southeast Asia. Food was cheap in the deltaic part of the region, thanks to high land yield, plentiful water and cheap transportation. The cost of maintaining a factory would be relatively low here.

The first major Bengal mission in 1633 had ended on the Orissa coast when the English set up a barely functional factory at Balasore. The entry into Bengal proper had to wait until 1656, and was made possible by the diplomatic initiative of Gabriel Boughton, an officer and surgeon in the employ of the Mughal court since 1645. The story goes that princess Jahanara, then thirty years old and unofficially the first lady of the court, was returning from her father's apartment to her own when her perfumed muslin garment caught fire from a candle. The ladies-in-waiting tried to save her, only to have their own clothes catch fire. Two of them died, but the princess survived, if just. In the next few months, Jahanara lay on what looked to be her deathbed, with a grief-stricken Shah Jahan constantly at her side. It remains a mystery how Jahanara was nursed back to health. In one version, Shah Jahan's prayers did the job. In another, Boughton's skills as a doctor worked. When offered a reward, Boughton sought a factory for the English in Bengal. Although this story and Bouhgton's medical acumen have been disputed, he probably did play a part in the negotiations that led to a factory. For Shah Jahan it was expedient to be well disposed to the English since he distrusted the Portuguese. He needed the former to fill in the vacuum left by the expulsion of the latter from Hooghly in 1632. The first factory of the

Company in Hooghly was followed by expansion of the Balasore factory and establishment of new factories at Kasimbazar and Patna.

Between 1660 and 1680, the Bengal enterprise grew, thanks to the interest the Company had developed in Dhaka muslins and Bihar saltpetre. But it was an uneasy growth. The problem was that Bengal was a different political entity from Coromandel or Surat. In Coromandel, Mughal authority was absent, and in Surat it had become precarious. But Bengal was an imperial province and governed firmly by a nobleman appointed by the imperial court. This the English realized at some cost in 1657, the year Shah Jahan died. Mir Jumla, the governor of Bengal and himself owner of trading vessels, was upset and made his displeasure known when the Company officers attempted to confiscate an Indian ship on account of an unpaid debt. Nothing untoward came out of this, as Mir Jumla was called away to deal with rebellions. But the Company learnt a lesson.

A new threat emerged in the 1670s. The reputation of Bengal as a promising commercial frontier and its proximity to the heart of the Mughal empire had drawn a large number of European private traders to settle down at the Ganges ports Kasimbazar and Hooghly. The very existence of a strong government encouraged these merchants to approach the Mughal viceroy Shaista

Khan, and his customs officer Balchandra Das, to seek trading rights, while offering in return duties at a higher rate than what the Company had negotiated with the emperor. Successful in negotiating with the local administration, the private traders moved around in Bengal in open defiance of the Company's authority. One Captain Ally travelled between Dhaka and Hooghly in a decorated and well-armed fleet, himself 'habited in scarlet richly laced', and developed 'great friendship' with Balchandra Das, much to the mortification of the Company.

Matters came to a head in 1682. In that year, the Company sent William Hedges as the governor in Bengal. Hedges' main commissions were to suppress private trade and to negotiate trade terms with Shaista Khan. The trade licenses that the Company received stated a percentage of customs to be collected on goods in transit both for import and for export. The standard rate was 3½ per cent of the value of the goods. But the European companies never willingly paid customs, nor made any commitments on this account. There were two reasons for the reluctance. First, the taxation rate was subject to uncertainty depending on wars, rebellions, or, simply, opportunism. Second, whereas on an investment of the Company in Bengal amounting to £600,000, the customs would come to £42,000, for 'half of which charge', the instructions from London told Hedges, it should be possible to arrive at a settlement with the king.

In short, the instructions asked the chief to bribe the nobility to keep the private traders out. But bribing was a game that the Company's rivals were willing to play to the hilt. Shaista Khan, then almost eighty years old and soon to retire from a glorious career, was not only well aware of the dilemma that the Company faced, but also took a mischievous delight in promising the Company concessions while secretly negotiating with its rivals. In the end, from 'the old doting Nawab', as Hedges angrily called him, the Company got nothing more than empty promises.

Not surprisingly, Hedges did not last long in his post. Though declared by the directors 'one of our own', his ego outstripped his understanding of Bengal politics. The most experienced Company officer in Bengal at the time was Job Charnock (1630–93). Charnock had served the Company in India for thirty years. He started his career in Hajipur and Patna, where he procured saltpetre, needed in England as raw material for gunpowder. In Patna, Charnock married an Indian widow said to have been rescued from burning herself on her husband's funeral pyre and had three children by her. While in Patna, he began to dress in Indian costumes, a habit that lasted lifelong, and learnt to speak fluent Persian and Hindustani. In 1669, he moved to the Bengal establishment in Hooghly where he was the fifth in the hierarchy of factors. In 1685, he became the second in command in Bengal.

Charnock had independent views and was effectively in charge of the Hooghly establishment by virtue of his personality and experience. He also had close links with the English private merchants of Kasimbazar. Therefore, he did not care for Hedges's leadership in the ongoing disputes over private trade and the Nawab. The directors dealt with the situation by removing Hedges, but blundered nevertheless. Believing that an agreement with the Mughal emperor held good in Bengal, they refused to negotiate with Shaista Khan, precipitating an open conflict. Although it was the last thing Charnock wanted, an armed conflict was forced on his small and inexperienced army by the belligerence of the London merchants.

In 1686, the Company in London, anticipating an outbreak of war in Bengal, sent a fleet to Hooghly. Additional troops were expected to come from Madras. The few hundred men who did join the Bengal troops were hardly a deterrent to the 40,000-strong Mughal forces. While the fleet was on its way, a series of skirmishes made Charnock worry for the safety of the people and the merchandise in Hooghly. He loaded the material and as many people as possible on country boats and sailed down the river. The party reached Sutanuti, where the Mughal forces caught up with them. Mughal heavy artillery, combined with the effects of disease and starvation, reduced numbers and morale on the English side. When all seemed lost, a Rajput noble Puran Mal (Baramal or Boremal in the sources) intervened to save the Company. The Mughal commander, moreover, was misinformed of the strength of the enemy forces and quickly accepted an offer of a truce. Charnock, in the negotiations that followed, made only one demand—the permission to build a fort in Bengal.

His dream came true three years later. These three years were turbulent for the Company's Bengal enterprise. A dispute over pirate attack upon pilgrim ships off the coast of Surat drew a severe reprisal from Aurangzeb, almost ending English presence in India in 1689–90. As peace was declared after an abject apology from the English, Aurangzeb sent a letter to the viceroy of Bengal, Ibrahim Khan, that the English, 'not being in their former greatness', may be pardoned and allowed to carry on in their small way in Bengal. Charnock's moment had finally arrived. In 1690, he returned to Sutanuti from exile in Madras to start the process of a zamindari sale. At the end of the negotiations, the Company became the zamindar of three villages, Sutanuti, Gobindapur and Dihi-Kalkutta, which right they purchased from the zamindars of the area, the Mazumdars, for Rs 1300.

Throughout this conflict, London wanted Bengal to be subordinated to the safer station at Madras. Charnock did not think that Madras could be relied on for armed relief to Bengal, nor considered Madras as a partner, for the two settlements, after all, competed for the same trade. Like Francis Day, he decided to go alone and build a fort with his own resources. Soon after Calcutta started, London, as usual, endorsed the decision and declared Charnock the governor of Bengal. Charnock enjoyed this dubious glory for three more years before he died. But years of stress had already taken a toll on his mind. He turned moody and disagreeable, withdrew from public affairs, let the management of the town go to seed, and lived in fear of being chased by Madras lawyers. He beat his servants and took great pleasure in encouraging intrigues and quarrels amongst his European staff. In this disorderly state of mind, one point of constancy was the memory of his dead Indian wife. He never failed to perform rituals, Indian style, on her grave on her death anniversary.

Historical evidence is unclear on the point of what

existed on the spot where Calcutta came up. Old Bengali accounts suggest that in the seventeenth century, the two banks of the river (Betor and Sutanuti) had textile markets that operated in certain seasons of the year. These fairgrounds were part sponsored by the Portuguese traders and may have grown as merchant settlements after the decline of Saptagram, the principal port of medieval Bengal. But it is very unlikely that these markets had a commercial future before the Company came in. No matter the prehistory, Calcutta quickly became a popular destination for Bengali merchants, and especially the textile merchants whom the Company and English private traders regularly dealt with. Many of them settled down in the new establishment or near it. The river had more water here than at Hooghly, even though it was also more treacherous in this spot. And Calcutta was easier for movement of troops from the sea if necessary.

With hindsight, it would be easy to credit Charnock with prescience unusual among Company officials in this time. Charnock was no visionary, however. He was only a merchant caught up in a complicated political scenario without enough military power, strategic resources, or the blessings of his superiors necessary to deal with the situation. He was one of many agents who had to fend for themselves. His decisions were taken on the spur of the moment and turned out to be right only after luck intervened in his favour. He was, however, special in one respect. In a world where working lives were quite short and most merchants and mariners chose not to spend many years in India, Charnock had adopted India as his home. Later biographers had difficulty piecing together his early life in London, which suggests that he had few ties with London and few reasons to return to England for. Surely he was not entirely exceptional in having lived the greater part of his life in India. There were other Englishmen who did too. But Charnock met a particular need. The political conditions of Bengal demanded a man who saw himself as a local rather than as the agent of a foreign firm. Charnock was such a man. It was his roots in Bengal that led him to ignore decrees issued by London and Madras.

A new world

The three new ports broke away from the Indian commercial mainstream in that they came up in new territories, away from the old ports that belonged to the Indian rulers. On the Coromandel, the new town came up in Madras rather than Masulipatnam, on the western coast in Bombay instead of Surat, and in Bengal the fort was erected in Calcutta rather than Hooghly or Kasimbazar, where the English already had a presence. This physical distance from the regimes in India was to prove far-reaching when the regimes became unstable in the eighteenth century.

The three towns also revealed a growing weakness within the Company. By the close of the seventeenth century, Bombay, Madras and Calcutta had a trading station and a fort each. The last one to come up was the Fort William in Calcutta. In every case, the construction of a fort was in defiance of orders from London. The directors based in the City did not comprehend India like the local administrators, who had a more practical understanding of the ground realities. The road for agents to become principals, if it had been open in 1600, was effectively blocked in 1690. There was, therefore, an unbridgeable mental distance between these two sets of people. The distrust arose not only from poor information about India in London, but also from a lack of appreciation of the local imperatives that decided the actions of the agents. Unable to control or reform the situation, the Company alternately praised and persecuted the most able of its factors abroad.

In the prevailing political atmosphere in England, the forts sometimes became symbols of royal power. Having forced a reluctant employer to grant them these havens of safety, the local agents often sided with the Crown. The new settlements became, in spirit, colonies of the king more than trading outposts. The Company did not try too hard to correct that impression. The heads of the establishments had been called agents before; after the restoration of monarchy, they were called presidents. In these newly acquired territories, the heads were also the governors. His Majesty's flag, the Union Jack, flew over buildings in these cities.

The town administration was recast in the London pattern, with a mayor and aldermen, of whom some were the Company's servants and the others Indian residents. These were the justices of peace, and wore ceremonial regalia on formal occasions. Silver gilt maces were carried before the mayor on these events. These justices presided over what became known as the mayor's court. The courts settled commercial disputes with reference to English common law. Indian merchants resorted to these courts and the laws, and not only out of necessity. In fact, writes the historian Kanakalatha Mukund in a recent book, 'the cosmopolitan character of traders who came to Madras and the emerging multi-racial society of the town . . . found the English court a great convenience.'

In 1687, the whole royalist paraphernalia caused a meeting to take place between the top brass of London and the king. A description of the meeting was later communicated to the governor of Madras Elihu Yale. In this meeting the king enquired if orders regarding administration of Madras ought not to come from him directly. To this question, the governor of the Company readily assented. But he insisted that the king refrain from making any appointments in his territories in India, for that would divide the authority there. The king reflected on this point and proposed that administrative orders could be passed by the Company in the name of the Crown. An important matter of policy was agreed upon—wisely it would seem in hindsight, for the king himself was deposed a year later.

The English fort in Bombay, 1703.
© National Maritime Museum, London.

GROWTH AMIDST TURMOIL

THROUGH THE MIDDLE decades of the 1600s, the Company needed to maintain a fine balance between the king and the Parliament. The turbulent years between the civil wars (1642–51) and the Glorious Revolution (1688) did not destroy the Company but increased uncertainty to such heights as to affect the disposition to make long term plans. During this period, a desperately cash-starved Charles I made several attempts to squeeze the Company for money. He finally succeeded in 1640 in the wake of the Scottish invasion. The king forced the Company to deliver 600,000 lbs of pepper on credit, sold the pepper in the market, raising £50,000 for himself. The goods were sold at a price lower than the one set by the Company and the loan was not repaid. The restored monarchy made good only a small part of the loss.

In the 1640s, the fluctuating fortunes of the royalists and their adversaries reduced the market for Indian produce. During Oliver Cromwell's rule, the rivalry in the Indian Ocean led to the First Anglo-Dutch War in 1652. At the peace negotiations of 1654, Cromwell succeeded in extracting the promise of compensation, little of which was actually paid. Cromwell also oversaw a renewal of the charter in 1657, which made the Company a permanent joint stock, thereby placing it on a firmer footing.

Nevertheless, political instability at home and conflicts abroad led the Company directors to tread a cautious path and they exhorted their agents to reduce employment and investment. There were two long term effects of the enforced caution. Firstly, the bane of the Company, the private traders, gained an advantage. Secondly, the weakness of the head office in London increased the discretionary powers of the branches and the men who managed them. While London called for restraint, the spirit of enterprise and aggression rose in India. The three new settlements embodied that assertive spirit.

These troubles at home form the theme of the present chapter.

Private trade and interlopers

London merchants with money to invest in a ship had reason enough, if not the sanctioned right, to make a trip to the Indian Ocean. On the Indian coast, they could openly engage in business as short-haul or 'country' traders. These merchants usually managed to find an officer of the Company on shore willing to enter into a partnership deal with them. The most attractive of such deals involved trade in some of the prohibited goods.

It was generally believed, and the Company never disputed the belief, that its employees were underpaid. The implicit understanding was that the employees would compensate themselves for their low salaries by engaging in personal trade, as long as it did not directly compete with the Company's business. The employees sometimes owned vessels of about 100 tons singly or in partnership. The ships bought goods along the coasts and plied between the Bay of Bengal littoral, Surat and Persia. Occasionally, when a large Company ship in need of repair or manpower was berthed in Calcutta for a whole year, the senior officers would use it for private coastal trade. The use of such resources went beyond what the Company would consider fair. The more powerful the officer the greater was the scope for free riding on the Company's resources. Almost anyone in a position of authority within the Company's agencies conducted some private trade. And that included the chaplains and the surgeons. This curious duality of service to Company and self aggrandizement followed by its officials made the Company unable to take a firm stand against private trade. It railed in public and pardoned in private.

On their part, many local officers thought the Company had little moral right to preach about good conduct. As Francis Day's case showed, private trade was not always opportunistic. Day built Fort St George with borrowed money, staking his personal reputation as a trader. John Weddell was a sea captain who had fought courageously for the Company but was fined and warned on account of private trade. Despite their remarkable contributions to the making of Bombay, both Oxenden and Aungier were disgraced on their return to England on charges of private trading. Elihu Yale had to leave the governorship of Madras on the same charges. But if Oxenden, Aungier, and Day could be persecuted, Thomas Pitt changed the rules of the game.

In 1674, a twenty-year-old merchant from Dorset reached the Company's settlement in Balasore and set up an independent trading concern in defiance of the Company's prohibition. Pitt was an extremely able entrepreneur and in a short time established a network of trade in sugar and horses spanning Persia and India. The Company ordered him to desist from trade, which he blithely ignored. With sagacity, he had married a relation of his local patrons, and the blessings of his Balasore in-laws allowed him to conduct business with impunity. In 1681, when Pitt briefly returned to England, court proceedings were initiated against him for sabotaging the Company's commercial interests. But before the ink had dried on the paper, Pitt was back in India to discuss with the Nawab of Bengal the prospects of securing a license to set up a factory. In 1684, he was arrested and an enforced exile followed. Again, he got away by paying a paltry fine, while using the imposed leisure to buy up land in Dorset and having himself elected to the Parliament in 1689. His career in the House of Commons saw a coordinated attack by the interlopers on the Company's monopoly in the East.

In 1693, Pitt returned to India. Again the Company tried to stop him without conviction or success. Eventually, in 1695, the Company directors changed strategy and offered Pitt the post of the president of Madras. Pitt happily accepted the offer. The subsequent turmoil in the Company elections showed how controversial the decision had been. The early part of his tenure of fifteen years in Madras led to a series of complicated diplomatic and military manoeuvers that brought peace and stability in the relations between the Company settlement and the Nawab of Carnatic. The latter part was taken up with the administration of Madras. Inevitably, Pitt got into trouble with his colleagues. One of the issues in the conflicts was interference by Company agents in the affairs of the Indian residents of the territory. Pitt had criticized a senior colleague for getting too involved in caste disputes. After protracted wranglings, Pitt was sent back to England in 1710.

The last fifteen years of his life were spent in managing his extensive estates, in Parliamentary activities, and in defending his right to possess one of the world's largest diamonds. This diamond he had acquired from a merchant in Madras in 1702. Forever a shrewd entrepreneur, Pitt had the diamond cut in England at huge expense, reducing it to one-third the original weight, but raising the price five-fold. The diamond was eventually sold in France, where it adorned Marie Antoinette's crown and Napoleon's sword, and is currently displayed in the Louvre.

Following Pitt's footsteps, interlopers became ever more prominent in business and public spheres. Thomas Bowrey, a private trader from a marine background, settled down in England after many years in the Bay of

Bengal as owner of merchant ships and became an authority on the Malay language. His most famous undertaking, a travelogue containing valuable details on contemporary Bengal, was rediscovered and published three hundred years after his death. Nathaniel Gould, one of the early governors of the Bank of England, began as an interloper in the 1690s. In the 1680s, John Child, a steadfastly loyal governor of Bombay accumulated considerable wealth by means of unconcealed private trade.

Pitt's example showed, furthermore, that the Company's claim to monopoly could be questioned.

The attack on monopoly

Influential members of the business elite complained that the Company benefited a small section of society by deliberately restricting the gains to a privileged coterie of shareholders. The point of the criticism was that the directors kept control of the Company by refusing to issue new stock. They arranged to raise loans, used the loans to finance trading investments, and made massive gains on the difference between interest rate and the profit on the India trade which was substantial. There was a cost attached to the strategy. The directors implicitly sacrificed any potential capital gains on their shareholdings. But they could well afford to give up such gains as the returns on their investments were extremely rewarding.

Attacks on the shareholders provoked counter-attacks. The leader of the counter-attack was Josiah Child (1630-99). A merchant and brewer, Child in his early life was a licensed private trader. In the 1670s, he assisted in the founding of the Royal African Company. With prudent political and economic moves, he emerged as the single largest shareholder of the East India Company by the end of the decade, and assumed leadership of the oligarchy of thirty-plus shareholders who took all decisions. Having overseen the issue of a new charter, Child started taking on the critics.

Child published a series of pamphlets under a pseudonym. The pamphlets made a case for continuing with monopoly in the Indian trade. He pointed out that the monopoly had been beneficial for the revenues of the state, and that the economies of scale had enabled the construction of larger and better ships. Answering the charge that the export of bullion for Indian goods was harmful for the nation, Child pointed out, rightly, that the real benefit was contained in the welfare effects of the cheap foreign goods that came in, and in the competitive edge established by England in overseas trade. Anticipating present-day critics of neo-liberalism,

Child voiced misgivings over the potential bad effects that 'unfettered' competition could bring about. He also pointed out that the trade needed military protection, which was best supplied by one large agency empowered by a royal edict.

As one would expect, Child's India policy, partly implemented through the Surat governor, his protégé and namesake John Child, saw more money being spent on local defence than before. Josiah Child was not alone in pursuing this course of action. The other principal shareholder, Thomas Cooke, who was a partner of Josiah in bribing the Court, endorsed a policy of aggression in India. Both these aspects of the old Company's activities became controversial in the wake of renewed political instability at home and a spat between Aurangzeb and John Child in Bombay.

The Glorious Revolution of 1688, which made the Dutch stadtholder William III the king of England, occurred at the same time as the Company had to battle a lobby of interlopers in the House of Commons. A number of moves were organized by those adversaries whom Child had angered during his leadership. They supported reissuing of stocks, limiting individual holding, even suggested the dissolution of the Company. The handloom weavers affected by imported Indian textiles declared their hostility to the Company. As the historian Alfred Plummer has shown, the weavers rioted when petitions to the Parliament for prohibition on the trade failed. A customs duty was imposed on Indian goods in response to their grievances, but the duty was hardly a check on the volume of demand. What strengthened the animosity was the public knowledge that the two richest corporate bodies in London, the City and the Company, were mainly employed 'for corrupting great men'. The old company paid generous bribes to ministers and officers who had influence in the court to defeat moves against it, paid the king himself £10,000, and offered him £50,000, which he refused.

A committee was set up by the House of Commons in 1693 to enquire into these allegations. The Committee sat in Leadenhall Street, sifted through volumes of ledger, and was mystified by an item of expenditure called 'special service' under which thousands of pounds had been spent, and the purpose of which the new governor Cooke alone understood. Suspicious contracts of saltpetre awarded to individuals close to the members of the Board were discovered. Although no money was found to have changed hands, the committee was informed that one of Cooke's trusted agents was sitting with a large sum of ready cash, clearly waiting for the storm to pass. Cooke was sent to prison pending a full confession. In the end, nothing came of the enquiry because a key witness to this transaction escaped abroad. But the Company had lost its moral right to a monopoly.

These developments had a complex effect on the role of the Crown in East India trade. The new arrangement reduced many of the royal prerogatives with respect to Parliament, but increased the monarch's say in matters concerning overseas trade. As we have seen, prominent interlopers had the backing of a lobby within the Parliament. And yet, throwing open the trade would amount to opposing the Crown that had issued the charter. The Crown continued to have an acute interest in the matter, because the East India trade was a huge source of tax revenue and a war with France had made this revenue even more keenly needed as the Crown found itself desperately short of money. The Company made a guaranteed payment to the state. There was a justified fear that private traders would escape paying any tax at all.

The compromise that emerged from a messy negotiation was a new East India Company in 1698, formed of the capital of prominent interlopers. The king allowed the new company to form, while respecting the old company's rights to prosecute individual interlopers. Both monopoly and competition, thus, were accommodated in a new charter. The resolution of the conflict was hardly ideological, though. While the old company bribed parliamentarians, the new company extended a cheap loan to the state, a burden it could ill afford to carry and which ensured its early death.

Even if the idea of monopoly had suffered, there was something to be said for a 'natural' monopoly, a single firm large enough to make use of the economies of scale in this business and to weather the still considerable risks. The old company possessed an array of forts, warehouses, ships, garrisons, vast capital, had access to thousands of artisans and merchants whom it did business with, and could offer the lure of dividends to scare away competition. The new company was starved of money, until the first instalment of interest became available on its extravagant loan. Eventually a merger was proposed, through the mediation of the treasurer, Sidney Godoplhin. His interest in pushing through the merger was fiscal in nature. The state needed money more acutely than ever before, and a single point of taxation of the profits of trade was better than two. In 1708, the rivals, then known as the English Company and the London Company, merged to form the United Company of Merchants Trading in the East Indies, which now became the holder of monopoly trading rights in the East.

The split had not changed things in India very much. There was a brief five years when the rival companies engaged in an embarrassing one-upmanship in India. Each carried the English flag, claimed to be the sole representative of the king, and asked the local rulers for trading privileges with the exclusion of the other. Murshid Kuli Khan and Azimusshan, the Bengal treasurer and viceroy respectively, took advantage of the competition and accepted gifts from both parties. The union left these recently concluded finanial deals in the lurch.

In the long run, the merger gave the Company an organizational stability that it had lacked through much of the seventeenth century. The capital of the Company was a fixed and definite sum, and the annual value of trade relatively stable, determined by an almost fixed shipping capacity. The conflict between the Crown and the Parliament, in which it had been caught in the last quarter of the seventeenth century, was a thing of the past. From time to time, the Company made loans to the public treasury to finance warfare. The Parliament returned the favour by not questioning the autonomy of the Company, and indeed authorizing it as a territorial power in its own right.

While peaceful relations continued between the state and the Company, the oceans were becoming more turbulent than before. During the seventeenth century, the number and the power of the 'privateers' had grown.

These were mercenary ships licensed by the state to carry arms and available for naval battles with foreign powers. When there was no battle, the privateers offered their services to private traders. And some of them roamed the seas in search of opportunities to attack cargo ships of foreign origin. A band of these sailors-merchants-pirates appeared off the coast of Surat in the last decades of the seventeenth century.

Piracy

In 1694, an English sea captain, Avory, raided a merchant ship belonging to the great Bohra merchant of Surat, Abdul Ghafoor. The raid upon the most important firm in western India laid bare a problem that had been growing for some time—the proliferation of European pirates. These mariners moved between private trade, plunder of ships on the high seas and service for the royal navy as privateers. Being simultaneously on the right and the wrong sides of the law, they could buy political protection with offer of a share in the profit from trade.

Avory's raids raised popular protest in Surat. The protests threatened to become violent, even posed a threat to the life of the president, were he not meanwhile arrested and kept in irons inside the state prison. The

Company got away by offering escort ships to accompany the haj-bound fleets. Two years later, Avory was followed by a more illustrious figure, William Kidd, a Scotsman who had spent the first forty years of his life in the West Indies and New York City in predatory pursuits. In 1696, he reached the pirate haven Madagascar. Thereafter, Kidd took a decision that was entirely unusual even for pirates of this time. He raided and robbed a ship returning from Mecca to India, loaded with rich Indian pilgrims. The 'brutality was extreme, and [the pirates] carried it so far as to violate several women of rank who were on board', reported Niccolao Manucci in 1707. Kidd probably thought he would get away without being identified, but the fleet was accompanied by a ship belonging to the Company, and it defended the party against the attack. Having been exposed, Kidd now openly prowled the west coast of India in search of prey and pillaged a number of French ships as well as friendly ones.

Aurangzeb held the English accountable for this, not without reason, for the Company representatives knew what was going on. But they did not do anything to stop it because some of the pirates, in their role as traders and privateers, helped the Company officials. Aurangzeb, however, did not take a very harsh stand against the British and his prime minister Asad Khan and naval officers diffused the threat to the Company. The dispute nevertheless unnerved the English, and they wrote frantic letters to the directors apprising them of the political risk that piracy posed for the official trading missions. These reports resulted in the sponsors of piracy to wash their hands off these episodes and deny their role. Kidd's own political sponsors either turned against him or were out of power when Kidd was captured, tried and executed in 1701.

A BRIDGE BETWEEN
MANY WORLDS

BETWEEN 1600 AND 1750, the trade between Indian merchants and artisans and European traders, backed by easier transportation between the two continents, led to major shifts in British consumption patterns. This era witnessed the Company pioneering the start of a European society in India. In the course of these changes, the Company had to deal with commercial crises and political upheavals. As K.N. Chaudhuri has shown, its resilience derived from three principal strengths, a bureaucracy, success in tapping Spanish silver, and the closer relationship it forged with the government.

As this chapter will show, the consequences of its consolidation as a trading and political power were far-reaching for India and for the world.

A consumer boom in England

The Company was the bridge between an unfolding pattern of mass consumption in Britain and tropical goods meeting that demand. The trend was disrupted by wars, plagues and fires. Even in the best of times, the boom was a very slow process by today's standards. Nevertheless, consumer welfare increased, for consumption expanded faster than the population of England. Extensive commercial infrastructure and institutions came into being, financed from the profits of overseas trade. Great merchant families emerged in London; ports, docks and warehouses were constructed, shipping freights fell, commercial laws were codified and shipbuilding became a big industry. Whole new generations acquired the skills—from navigational to linguistic to financial—that served foreign trade.

Banking and insurance expanded to make London, with Amsterdam, the financial capital of Europe. One development of great importance was the bill discounting business. In the eighteenth century, trade credit instruments began to be widely used across firms, countries and continents. Bankers joined the boards of merchant companies. The Bank of England (1694) functioned as a 'lender of last resort' and banker to the state. Together with the Company, it formed the core of the emerging financial markets and supported the military-fiscal regime of the Hanoverian monarchs. These institutions were later to serve the Industrial Revolution. Whereas in the early eighteenth century, industrial firms rarely did business on credit, in the early nineteenth century, the large factories routinely followed the system. Their ability to accept credit depended on the soundness of the bill discounting business that had already been in existence. That ability made it possible for Manchester to sell textiles across the world.

In different times, different goods led the consumer boom. Asian pepper was the leading article in the first half of the seventeenth century. The medieval Europeans were ready to spend fortunes and risk lives for black pepper—and cinnamon, ginger, saffron, nutmeg, clove, mace and galangal, more or less in that order. Why pepper was so coveted a good is still not fully understood. It was once thought that spices were used as preservatives, or worse, to hide the smell of stale meat. In a recent book, Paul Freedman questions this notion. Having consulted many old cookbooks written in several languages, he concludes that spices were a status symbol, a luxury rather than a necessity, the more sought after because of their association with the exotic East. In the second half of the century, two American products, tobacco and sugar, were added to the basket of leading imports. As the cost of production in the Virginian plantations fell drastically, the price of tobacco in 1700 fell to one-twentieth the 1620 price, and the import increased from below 20,000 to 22 million pounds. West Indian sugar production and import began to expand late in the seventeenth century, and continued on a similar trajectory through much of the early eighteenth century.

By 1700, two products from India dominated the Company's imports, cotton cloth and saltpetre. Two general types of cloth entered the European market—chintz or printed textiles, and calicoes or bleached cloth. The particular attraction of coloured cloth had less to do with the cloth itself, and rather more with the range of exquisite natural dyes that were used to colour them. Moreover, decorative technologies like blocks, embroidery and hand-painting or kalamkari were already highly developed in India. Eventually, Indian prints began to define the standards of fashion in Europe.

In 1700, the total textile import by all European companies from India amounted to 25-35 million square yards. Britain took about two-thirds this quantity. Despite Parliamentary acts trying to restrain the trade, there was little change in volume in the next one hundred years; in 1790–1800, the average quantity imported from India into Britain was still 22 million yards. Although some of this import substituted domestic production, much of it came in as additional consumption. If the population in Britain was 5 million in 1700, the cloth imported from India would amount to 5 yards per person, which was possibly a quarter to a third of the total consumption of cloth per person.

The last Asian product to feed the consumption boom was tea. Tea-drinking in England became a mass habit from early in the 1700s. The quantity of tea brought into Britain was less than a million pounds in 1728. In 1755, three million pounds came in. 'Where will this evil stop?' asked a worried pamphleteer in 1757. In the 1770s, anywhere between four and seven million pounds of tea were being imported, much of it smuggled. Smuggling was unstoppable because tea was one of the most heavily taxed consumer items. It was the repeal of the tea taxes in response to the smuggling, and the imposition of compensatory taxes on re-exports of tea to the American colonies, that led to the Boston tea party in 1773.

The consumer boom was not just a by-product of the great expansion in overseas trade. Rather, as the historian J.R. Ward suggests in an article, the two developments reinforced one another. While trade transformed British society, mass consumption of traded goods encouraged overseas trade. This effect could be seen most clearly in the case of tea. The Company's expansion into China in the eighteenth century owed indirectly to the growth of an urban working class in Britain, and the fast-growing habit of drinking tea. Anybody who cared for the poor would be in favour of overseas trade.

What made the wheel of trade go round was American silver.

Treasure from the Americas

The Spanish conquest of the Americas made silver cheaper in Europe than in Asia. The Company repeatedly tried to pay for Indian goods with European goods. Except woollen textiles to a small extent, no other export succeeded in India until late in the eighteenth century, when the Indians began buying a lot of iron goods from Britain. Until then, demand in India and European manufacturing capability did not match well at all. The Company's purchases in India, therefore, depended on access to silver as a means of payment. The decision to export bullion owed also to the high cost of borrowing money in India. Interest rates were much higher in India than in western Europe, and it made sense to import capital into India

The export of bullion made the Company's position in the City of London politically insecure. The currencies of the time were all metallic, and gold and silver were in great demand everywhere as means to balance trades. Under these circumstances the Company's annual procurement in order to finance the India trade caused widespread concern about balance of trade in other fronts. Reactions from the many critics of the firm threatened to become violent when news came that the Company had become drawn into fighting battles in India, as in the time of John Child's tryst with the Mughal army.

Improvements in shipping and the knowledge of shipping routes also aided trade and settlement.

The journey

Travel by an East Indiaman, the ship that carried personnel and cargo for the European East India Companies, changed between 1600 and 1750.

The very first voyages had been exploratory, in that they stopped in a number of places to test commercial prospects, and therefore could take almost two years to reach India. These trips were constantly plagued by accidents. This is best shown with the example of one early journey. The fourth voyage of the Company, in which John Jourdain was a passenger, set off in March 1608. In May, the voyagers stopped at the Canary Islands and the Cape Verde Islands to pick up water, grain and goats and proceeded on a non-stop run for five weeks to reach the Cape in July. On the way, they passed one Portuguese carrack and a Dutch ship, itching to pick up a fight. Devastated by scurvy, the crew rested in Cape for two months, while the ships were refitted for the stormy waters that awaited them. In September they set off again, losing sight of two ships in a violent storm. One of the ships caught up with them in Aden months later, the other one had a miserable time trading in Sumatra and returned broke to England. In November 1608, the main ship, looking for Zanzibar, reached Pemba on the East African coast. Here skirmishes broke out between the local merchants and the Europeans, and the ships fled the port.

A period then followed when the party floundered facing the northeast monsoon winds against them. The ship carrying food was lost. In January 1609 the famished crew reached a group of islands, possibly the Seychelles. These islands turned out to be a 'paradise on earth'. Fish, fowl and the delightful fruit 'coker nutt' were there in plenty. There were also many small crocodiles, which were unusually tame, not having encountered hungry European sailors before, and were easily caught, killed and eaten. After a month of rest and recovery here, they set off to reach Aden, only just making it by forcing a Gujarati ship captain to show them the way. In Aden, English iron and broadcloths found buyers, but not before much cunning bargaining mixed with veiled threats of murder and imprisonment. In July 1609, the ship sailed for the Gulf of Cambay. The monsoon winds again blew them off course to Kathiawar. It was not before September, after losing the main ship, that the crew reached Surat, to find that the Portuguese had forbidden the town administration to allow them entry. In the first decade of the seventeenth century, most expeditions moved in a similarly unpredictable fashion.

Between 1620 and 1750, innovations and improvements in shipbuilding reduced the journey time by an East Indiaman. The journey was much shortened. Ships more than doubled in size. Earlier, the small size meant that an extra ship was necessary to carry food and water and frequent stops had to be made for replenishment of supplies. If the ship carrying the provisions was lost, as in the fourth voyage, there would be famine on board. Now, food and water went with the passengers. Local pilots were not necessary any more. Shorter time at sea reduced the incidence of scurvy. The monsoon wind was used more efficiently than before. Victualling stops were fewer and further between. Instead of the Canary Islands or the Cape Verde, the ships leaving London stopped at Madeira to pick up wine, which was in great demand among Europeans in India. The second long halt was at the Cape, where ships halted for repairs. From Cape to Calcutta, the two stops at Zanzibar and Aden were replaced with a more convenient stop at the Comoro Islands or Madagascar. In less than six months in all, the passengers would be in sight of Balasore, reaching the mouth of the Hooghly the next morning.

The factory

The centre of the Company's operations in India was the factory, known as the aurung in Bengal. The factory was not a place for production, but a warehouse where goods were delivered, sorted, inspected and stored. It was run by a council. Apart from the chief, the main functionaries of the council were the accountant, the storekeeper, the purser marine and the secretary who kept minutes of all meetings, then known as 'consultations'. The secretary also prepared a general review of the work of the factory and sent a copy of the consultations, along with this review, to the directors in London. These documents constitute the main resources used by historians. The chaplain and the surgeon were also prominent members of the factory set-up, and were the intellectual face of European society in India. After these officials in the pecking order was the steward.

Below the administration, there were a large number of merchants, factors, writers, clerks and apprentices.

Ordinarily, the office work was light, and completed in three hours during the morning, and three hours in the afternoon, with a long lunch break in between. But when ships arrived or departed, the office would be extraordinarily busy for a few days. Officers on the Company's pay lived a regulated life, rather like that in an old university town. They had free quarters in the factory, and had a number of servants and attendants. The chief officers were also permitted to use palanquins. When moving about, they were accompanied by a group of European soldiers, and, sometimes, town-criers. The officers never ventured more than a mile or two from the factory. The furthest they usually went was the garden at the edge of the town. Here, if the location were Surat or Hooghly, the Dutch officers would join the English in the mornings and evenings for a friendly walk together.

Lunch usually took place on the public table, and was a lavish affair. European cooks were in demand, and the European factories keenly competed for their services. Wines and spirits were desperately in short supply. The best wines were imported, and reserved for the officers. Meals were usually accompanied by locally brewed spirits. A whole system of brewing developed to make

Indian raw material into a tolerable, if at times dangerous, drink. Hierarchy and formality were maintained in the seating order. And yet, as soon as the juniors found themselves alone, they dressed themselves in Indian robe and pyjamas, reclined upon the carpet to enjoy the meal Indian fashion, and, as the traveller Niccolao Manucci informs us, chewed paan and smoked hukkah afterwards.

Despite the outward show of regulation and moderation, life in the factory nurtured covert violence. The factors competed with each other professionally and personally. They had their clerks and apprentices spy on each other. The brazenness with which private trade was conducted gave the factory an air of corruption. Competition over women, and the unconvincing attempts at recreating an aristocracy, led to quarrels. Early documentation of daily life is replete with stories of duels fought on trivial issues. Near Alipur bridge in Calcutta stood two trees, known as the 'trees of destruction', for the number of duels fought under it, almost all of them over rivalry in love. In such conditions, the chaplains played a crucial role in instilling some moral order. The personality of the chaplain, therefore, made a large difference to the quality of life.

The expenses of the local establishments were a source of concern for the London office. The instructions stipulated that the local expenditure was to be funded by local revenues. But there were numerous avenues of corruption and wastage. Besides, London authorities did not fully understand the accounts. The chief officers recreated the pomp of an Indian royalty and employed far too many retainers. The governor is 'respected as a Prince by the Rajas of the country'. He had the privilege of owning horse carriages and palanquins. He went out on business surrounded by dozens of peons and English guards, two of them carrying the Union Jack before his palanquin, Indian agents on both sides fanning him to drive the flies away, and a band of Indian musicians playing 'Country Musick enough to frighten a stranger' (Charles Lockyer, 1711).

Food and drink allowances provided an opportunity for 'debauchery'. During a special dinner in early eighteenth-century Madras, one lamb dish cooked in the Mughal style and containing a liberal quantity of ambergris cost 200 rupees to make, over a hundred thousand rupees in today's money. Ships owned by the Company's servants were unofficially given a discount on the port duties. Allowance for buying gifts for the local notables supplied ways to pilfer money.

Much of our knowledge of life inside the factory comes from the consultations books.

The consultation book

The consultation books recorded everything that happened in the factory. What kind of events did they record? A snapshot based on the Masulipatnam book covering the period July 1682–December 1683 should be representative.

Consultation books were logbooks, devoting about a page on the affairs of each day. Some days were left blank because nothing happened. Of the subjects written about, if we exclude descriptions of quantities and prices of goods bought, there were perhaps three main topics. The routine or mundane included ships' arrivals, advance news of ships, arrival of agents from other factories, negotiations with bankers on rates of exchange, negotiations with transporters and 'washermen' who processed cloth and, of course, reports of meetings ('discourses') with cloth merchants and agents. These subjects required no more than a few sentences. At a more serious and policy level were three issues: negotiations between the factors and the governor of the town and his emissary the 'Eminent Merchants', dealing with interlopers and settling contractual disputes with the cloth merchants. There was finally another head, under which were dealt contingencies like death, disease or sudden arrivals. Thus a prosaic account of receipts and payments would suddenly take a philosophical turn and ponder on the frailty of human life. The humdrum routine was also broken when on occasions like a monsoon day in 1683, a ship from Bengal deposited the family of John Aelst, an unknown adventurer who wanted to set himself up as a diamond merchant.

The policy discussions were the most consequential. The governor Mahmud Ali Beg, from time to time, sent polite requests to the factory asking to buy cases of wine, spirits and sugar. The factory sent the goods to him, politely withholding the bill. This practice 'the Councell Esteeme much the Cheaper way' to maintain good relations. As the season changed, and interloper ships appeared on the horizon, it became clear what service these gifts were expected to buy. On 17 August 1683, a ship named Constantinople under John Smith lost its way in strong wind and came ashore. On board were 'two Jews one named Rodriques the other Deporta'. The factory's spies informed that 'John Smith and two Jews' were about to meet the governor. The factory promptly sent a retinue of agents to the governor's court to dissuade him from meeting them. The governor's goodwill was crucial in catching and prosecuting interlopers, a task that the factory had difficulty doing on its own. The governor, in turn, was reluctant to be seen as a patron of the English Company in exclusion of all the other merchants of the town. On one occasion when the factors made a present and asked for help in apprehending an interloper, a plainly irritated Mahmud Ali refused the present, and 'in a jeering way advised that one of us might go upto Court and get all interlopers defeated'. This setback was met with an order to all Indian agents to forthwith bribe the officers of the court.

The interlopers made the Company's job of negotiating with Indian merchants a difficult one. On 20 November 1683, a heated argument took place with the Indian suppliers on account of a large consignment that was rejected for poor quality. The merchants refused to take back the cloth and threatened that they would henceforth 'seek another market'. The Council retired for a private consultation and returned to the table, meekly accepting all demands having 'thought best to humour them'. The reason for ready acquiescence was obvious—interloper ships had been spotted by the spies.

On a more day-to-day basis, the subject of dialogue was contract fulfilment and the quality of goods delivered. With a ship waiting to be loaded, the contract orders needed to be met quickly, but the merchants were found 'very shie in contracting for an Investment in soe short a time'. The factors' job was to have them 'smartly discoursed thereabout' in accepting the contract.

Too often, merchants appeared daunted by the prospect of undertaking 'so large an Investment as the like was never knowne before in this place.' Inevitably, when the contracted time came to receive delivery upon such order, the council had to 'express themselves very greatly disgusted' by the delays. Another area where problems arose related to quality and design of the goods. Printed and painted cloths often came in samples at first, but were found either over-priced or 'not with that Curiosity and Workemanship as desired', again requiring much negotiation and lengthy discourses.

European society

In 1720, a rough count showed that in Bombay, the factory population consisted of eighty employees and merchants, all men, about twenty-six women, nearly all of them married, eight children, and fifty soldiers. The numbers are not large, but they do not include the unspecified number of soldiers who had been dismissed from service, merchants who had left the factory to start private business and employees who had completed indentures and stayed on as traders. The numbers do reflect the hugely imbalanced demography of the factory population, as indeed was the case with many migrant merchant groups in this time. The average worker was a junior officer or factor, a male in his twenties. If fortunate and enterprising, he could hope to complete an indenture with the Company without falling sick or dying, make enough money on the side, and then either return home to a life of ease, or stay on to improve his fortunes as a private trader. Until that moment of freedom, the hierarchy between the officers and the subalterns could become oppressive and the boredom of a clerk's life too great to bear.

The temptation, then, to leave this prison and go out into the world was irresistible. But what was there outside the walls? The European sailors and soldiers formed a society quite distinct from those of the European factors, especially the higher officers. The two groups rarely socialized. The sailors' lives were less orderly and subject to the uncertainty of warfare and climate. When ship repairing, an ongoing conflict, or simply the want of sufficient hands stranded a ship on shore, the sailors lived in the midst of a makeshift Indian settlement. This was the society outside the factory.

Liquor and women best symbolized the social distance between the senior factory officers on one side, and the poorer merchants, sailors and soldiers at the other end of the spectrum. Europeans faced the constant problem of securing alcoholic drinks in India, arguably the least friendly country in the world to pursue such a project. The chief officers of the factory had access to imported wine and spirits. Madeira was brought into India by the crate-load, but was reserved for the bosses. Others procured their drinks in India. From sheer desperation, they drank almost anything anywhere. 'Several Europeans lose their Lives by the immoderate use of tempting Liquors', wrote Captain William Symson in 1715. He was referring to the fermented palm toddy of Surat. In the second half of the eighteenth century, the situation had improved only to the extent that a number of shore-side pubs were in operation in all the trade settlements, notably in Calcutta. But the quality of the drinks they served remained as dreadful as before. The main drink was 'bowl punch', a cocktail made out of arrack, jaggery, lemon juice and a squeeze of muscadine. The drink was thought to be the reason for the rapid decline in health and the consequent high mortality rate of European sailors waiting for a ship.

In the Lalbazar area in central Calcutta, where the police headquarters were located, about 1770 there had developed a cluster of 'low taverns' owned by Italian, Spanish and Portuguese characters. These places served 'paria arrack to the great debauchery of the soldiers'. Before these 'punch houses' and 'arrack houses' were regulated, pubs called Harmonic, Union, Wright's New

Tavern, Exchange, Crown and Anchor represented the real international face of Calcutta. A Bengali book published in 1915 stated that the ruined front of one of these pubs could still be seen on the old Kolutolla Street; a plaque showed the date when it started, 1767. Serving alcohol was always a legal business. As early as 1720, we know of a Bibi Domingo Ash, possibly an Indo-Portuguese, acquiring the license to distribute arrack in Calcutta. Yet, the pubs acquired a bad reputation that attached to the whole European working class of the city. They were sites of violent brawls and murders. One reason for the violence was that both European and Indian river-pirates sold the plundered goods in these pubs, and there were disputes over the sales. But the quality of the drink must have added to the foul mood.

Few of the employees could get the chance to marry European women. Even among the officer elite, the presence of European women often caused more duels than marital alliances. Nor did the officers and employees appear too fussy about the ethnicity of partners in the seventeenth century. There was even a positive preference for Indian women, and possibly some competition between the European nationalities for local women. 'The rich exuberance of the country,' François Bernier wrote in the 1680s, 'together with the beauty and amiable disposition of the native women, has given rise to a proverb in common use among the Portuguese, English, and Dutch, that the Kingdom of Bengale has a hundred gates open for entrance, but not one for departure'. The interest was just as lively a century later. Otherwise a severe critic of the Bengalis, the Dutch officer John Stavorinus (1770) softened on the subject of Bengali women, and acknowledged that they were 'well-proportioned', even if 'uncommonly wanton'. Indian women were 'much admired by the European gentlemen', wrote another contemporary. The specially coveted ones were the 'ladies of the Gentoo cast', being 'so exquisitely formed, with limbs so divinely turned, and such expression in their eyes', etc. (Philip Stanhope, 1784). A merchant of Calcutta in the 1780s, Bartholomew Burgess wrote a whole treatise on the many uses of the veil, pragmatic and romantic, of 'the Indostan female'.

Lyrical as the sentiment was, no woman of the Brahmin and the merchant classes was available to the Europeans. For, 'the Rich Merchants make Sure to marry their children before they come to 8 years of age' (Thomas Bowrey, 1670). And as for the grown-up women of the wealthy classes, 'their seclusion from society is . . . most rigidly adhered to' (William Tennant, 1804). The elite among the Indians, whether Muslim or

Hindu, shut the door of their inner social circles firmly in the face of the Europeans.

When the Europeans sought Indian women, they came to the shore-side townships that had a ready supply. In the 1770s, the northern suburb of Calcutta Baranagar had become famous 'on account of the great number of ladies of pleasure' plying their trade under license issued by the Dutch company (Stavorinus). Some befriended the dancing girls and had to suffer their 'exceedingly annoying' music as punishment. Others socialized in the sprawling slums outside the white factory towns and mixed with the artisans and other working people. A large number, of course, took mistresses from the same pool. An account of the daily life of the typical English merchant of Calcutta in 1770 notes matter-of-factly that at eight in the morning when the head attendant enters the master's bedroom, 'a lady quits his side' and either takes a private staircase to go upstairs or is conducted out of the premises, as the case may be.

The attempts to bypass the rigidities of Hindu society produced some touching moments. William Hickey, attorney, socialite and one of the richest citizens of Calcutta in the 1780s, in his memoirs referred to his companion as 'my little' sweeper-woman. But in the larger expatriate English community, the result of these choices was a hardening of caste sentiments among the ruling class, members of which were rich and powerful enough to marry European women. All alliances between the English and Indian women were looked down upon. The children of such alliances, often successful artisans and merchants themselves, were barred from government and military positions until the mid-nineteenth century.

One of the first tasks of a newly-appointed priest was to consecrate marriages and baptize children (even the wives) with retrospective effect. We know very little on the relationship between the European son-in-law and his Indian relatives. Whereas for the officers, we can assume they kept their Indian relatives at an arm's length, many sailors and soldiers in the late 1700s did in fact live in the 'black' townships.

Partly owing to these alliances, the social exclusiveness of the factory premises was fast disappearing in the eighteenth century. A substantial class of European and Indo-European artisans, traders and soldiers lived in the Indian quarters. Many Europeans sought service with the Indian princes, usually as mercenary soldiers, and they needed to engage socially with the courtiers and Indian soldiers. At the same time, more European women than before had begun sailing to India in the hope of marrying the 'nabobs'. As the officer and the administrative class had greater access to European women, the sailors, traders and soldiers who married working-class Indians were pushed closer to the Indian society. The inevitable effect of the dual trend was the effort to racially downgrade the Indo-European mixed population in the nineteenth century. Mimicking the Indian upper castes, the European ruling elite treated marriage beneath the caste, in this case non-Whites, as a ground for social exclusion. In a curious reversal of roles, instead of fallen women, the society was creating thousands of fallen men, whose lower social status was cemented by exclusion from superior jobs that were reserved for those born of purer alliances.

Historians of Indo-European society (Percival Spear, P.J. Marshall, and, more recently, Durba Ghosh) have usually approached their subject from the angle of European ideas of race. But Indian ideas of purity and pollution formed an older and no less powerful a sentiment than race. The effect of these ideas in shaping hierarchy in this hybrid world remains unstudied.

East India Company factory, Sonargaon, Bangladesh, from the Archaeological Survey of India Collections, taken by W. Brennand in 1872. © Piyal Kundu and http://oldindianphotos.blogspot.com/

PARTNERS AND AGENTS

AMONG THOSE INDIAN businesses and tradesmen that came in close contact with the European merchants between 1650 and 1850, five main classes deserve special attention. These were the great banking firms, merchants and shipwrights, officers and agents of the Company, artisans, and Indian partners of European private traders. There were also transporters, boatmen, caravan-runners and numerous other peoples besides who did business with the Europeans, but we have little systematic knowledge about these groups.

Who were the principal partners and agents of the Company in India?

Bankers

The most prominent urban capitalists of the seventeenth century were the bankers and money-changers, known as shroffs, kothiwals, mahajans, pedhis and other epithets. Money was scarce throughout India, and it was not surprising that bankers were the wealthiest capitalists. Few of these firms were deposit bankers. They brokered financial services required by the Company. The bullion for payment of Indian goods was imported in the shape of Spanish silver coins. The bankers arranged to have them recoined for a fee, or simply exchanged the peso for Indian money. The Company needed the moneylenders to borrow money when bullion ran out and convert the currency of one kingdom into that of another. In the eighteenth century profits and revenues earned in Bengal were sent to the other branches by means of bankers' drafts, or hundi. The major operators in the hundi market were the Indian bankers.

The beginning of British rule had an ambivalent impact upon this class. With increasing unification of currency and coinage, the British needed them less than before for financial transactions like currency exchange and conversion. Thus illustrious bankers like Jagatseth of Bengal found the ground shifting beneath their feet under Company rule. On the other hand, new areas brought under the British fold enjoyed greater security of property that encouraged general trade and finance. The acquisition of Benares by the Company in 1775, for example, improved the commercial importance of the city and that of its capitalists. This indirect stimulation to Indian business found its most flourishing expression not only in the interior towns such as Benares, but more significantly in the three port cities of Bombay, Madras and Calcutta.

Merchants

The rise of Indo-European trade did not happen at the expense of Indian traders. It was quite the opposite, in fact. The ports where the Europeans had their stations were located too far away one from the other. The companies' own shipping lines were insufficient to create necessary links between these ports, and between them and the smaller coastal markets where useful goods were available. This sphere of subsidiary or feeder supplies, called country trade, engaged a large number of Indians as well as Europeans. When the Company reduced its trading operations towards the end of the eighteenth century, the country traders moved into India-China trade.

Among merchants and shipwrights who gained from the European presence, the Parsis were the foremost. The Parsis had settled as agriculturists and artisans in towns on the south Gujarat coast before 1600. European trade drew some of these families to Surat. With the growth of Bombay, some of the prominent Parsi families left Surat for Bombay. Members of this community would go on to achieve pre-eminence in the business, social and cultural spheres in the coming decades. Among the foremost entrepreneurs of these times were Framji Cowasji Banaji and Rustomji Cowasji, shipwrights of nineteenth-century Bombay and Calcutta, the founder of the mill-owning Dinshaw Petit firm, Nasserwanjee Cowasjee Bomanjee, and K.R. Cama, who partnered with Dadabhai Naoroji to set up a merchant firm in Liverpool.

The golden age of Parsi shipwrights and coastal merchants began towards the end of the eighteenth century and continued well into the nineteenth. Not only trade but also wars with China and Burma helped them as they supplied provisions to the army. The rising price of oak in Europe made Burma and Malabar teak a cheaper material to use in shipbuilding. The Parsis knew the coastal timber trade better than did the European traders. When the Company's charter ended in 1833, a number of large ships were sold to the Parsis at a discount price which aided the coastal trading enterprise. Above all, Indian shipbuilding owed to the inherited skills of the Indian shipwright. Although the ships were on average smaller than the Europe-bound vessels, they were known to last a very long time.

Compared to Bombay, the shipbuilding trade was

less developed in Madras and Calcutta. But these cities too saw flourishing country trade. In Coromandel, the principal Indian groups dealing with the Company were the Telugu merchants who had migrated southward with the consolidation of power by the Telugu warlords. Many of them settled in Madras, and some in Pondicherry. Troubled conditions in the southern Deccan encouraged migration of weavers and merchants into the city. The weavers' quarters, Chintadripet, was a settlement that dates from the 1730s. These traders engaged in trade on their own account as well as in agency of the Europeans.

Like the Parsis, a group that thrived almost solely on the strength of their position in Indo-European trade was the Armenians. From their base in Julfa Isfahan, Armenian merchants had come to India in the sixteenth and seventeenth centuries. Their reputation as traders made them respectable citizens of the merchant town. The Armenian settlement in Madras began about 1700. In the eighteenth century, they used their contacts in Persia to juggle between overland and maritime trade off the coast of Persia, and obtain silver from Manila for Madras.

Calcutta grew as a haven of private enterprise by drawing in Bengali, Parsi, Gujarati and Marwari businesses. That Calcutta was relatively sheltered from the threat of Maratha attacks by the Company's forces made it an attractive destination for capitalists and entrepreneurs of the mid-eighteenth century. Bengali textile merchants, Seths and Basaks, were among the early wealthy Indian settlers of Calcutta. Some of these families had migrated from Saptagram when the river port there began silting up. The early families were called 'jangalkata', clearers of forest. Some of the oldest localities, markets and bathing ghats in Calcutta (Sovabazar, Baishnabghata, Burrabazar) were named after these merchants or were started by them.

In the last quarter of the eighteenth century, Bengali merchants of the Suvarna Banik caste became prominent in trade. For instance, Nemaicharan De-Mullick, Ramkrishna Mullick and Gangabishnu Mullick traded in opium and salt, successfully though perhaps not at the same level as the Parsi merchants. At the turn of the nineteenth century, the confederation of prominent Indian merchants had diversified further to include individuals who had no previous experience in trade. Prankrishna Laha and Matilal Seal were the big names among several rags-to-riches stories.

A junior employee of one of these firms, Ramdulal Dey stands out as a most dramatic case of making a fortune from very humble beginnings. Dey was a Bengali merchant, philanthropist and social leader, and benefactor of the greatest educational institution of early colonial Calcutta, the Hindu College, later the Presidency College. Having lost all during the Maratha raids in western Bengal in the 1740s, his parents settled in Calcutta and lived in poverty. While a teenager, Dey joined as a clerk one of the firms that supplied goods to European private traders. As an employee he showed evidence of entrepreneurial talent and extraordinary courage. Bengali children still read the story of how, returning home alone through forested roads with a large amount of money on his person, he fooled a band of robbers into thinking that he was a tramp of unsound mind. Dey's meteoric rise in the 1790s owed to his status as the principal agent of the American trading ships in Calcutta. The Philadelphia merchants honoured him by naming a ship Ramdulal.

With a few exceptions, all of these Bengali merchant firms invested their profits in buying landed estate, which perhaps explains why a trade recession in the 1840s saw some of them withdraw from trade and become full-fledged landlords.

Agents and officers

Till the early decades of the nineteenth century, a few Indian officers were hired by the Company to act as informants. They kept the Company updated on the goings-on in the political field. Variously known as vakyanavis, hurkurra or vakeel, their relevance to European business was indirect, and this too declined after the last Anglo-Maratha Wars ended in 1818. Thereafter, the intrigues in the princely states concerned the Company less than before and were monitored directly by resident representatives.

A more important person was the salaried agent in charge of procuring goods. When the Company began operations in India, the chief agents were powerful political figures with influence in the local courts. In Coromandel, they were usually in command of a band of soldiers, and thanks to this militia, could undertake contracts to collect land revenue on behalf of weak kings. With the establishment of Madras, Bombay and Calcutta, the character of the brokers changed. They were more often individuals with superior financial resources commanding a good credit in the Indian market. They were recruited from the very groups that were already established in the commercial world of coastal India. The agents of the Company in Calcutta were recruited from the families of the Seths and Basaks; those in Murshidabad were north Indian merchants; those in Madras were the Telugu merchants; and the chief agents in Surat were usually Parsis.

The agents were a diverse group, but two types can be identified. One was a sort of secretary to the European factor, known as dubash (dubashiya or interpreter) in the Coromandel and banyan in Bengal, and the second was a head merchant with whom the Company contracted for the supply of goods, usually known as 'broker'. Frequently, these roles merged in one individual. Europeans, in almost all dealings with the Indians, preferred to elevate one man over others. If this practice made contracting simpler, it left a large number of ambitious and aspiring merchants unhappy. The consultations and diaries of the time are replete with endless bickering over how brokerage should be shared between the bigger and the smaller merchants.

The best-known of all dubashes, somewhat disappointingly for the historian of the English Company, was an agent of the French. This gentleman, Ananda Ranga Pillai, kept a diary. For the most part, the diary is a tedious account of Pillai's relations with his kindred and family. Pillai, nevertheless, reveals some of the pros and cons of working for the Europeans. Half the French Company's trade in the 1740s passed through his hands, and so did the private trade of the leading officers. By his own admission, in order to maintain this empire, he had to employ so many subcontractors spread over so large an area, that his profits were small. Yet, 'from Cape Comorin [to] Bengal, . . . Golconda, and . . . Mysore, there is not one who is not [his] friend, and there is none who will not honour [his] drafts and bonds.' Alliance with a firm far larger in size than any Indian business of the time created a tremendous goodwill for an Indian merchant though the financial rewards may not have been sizeable.

Still, the relationship between the agent and the Company was far from an easy one. It was a relationship mired in dependence and distrust. It soured too easily and too frequently. There were many reasons for the relationship to sour. One of these is revealed in Pillai's complaint that he needed to spend too much money trying to hold an empire of under-contractors together. Another bone of contention related to debts to the Company owed by the deceased predecessors in Indian merchant firms. Under Indian custom, the liability of such loans was open to dispute. By European law, the liability passed on to the next generation. These loans, therefore, were occasions for furious quarrels. A third problem was conflict of interest. In places like Hooghly or Masulipatnam, local merchants were often placed in an awkward position when the Company seemed at odds with the kings. In 1678–79, the dubash of Masulipatnam, Kola Venkadri, secretly negotiated with the king of Golconda, and was imprisoned by the English in retaliation. Brokers who belonged in different communities used their leverage with the Company as a weapon to score over each other. The rivalry between the Parsi and Hindu merchants of Surat revolved around the Company. When a debt dispute arose between the Bombay Council and Jagannath Laldas, the leading Hindu merchant of Surat and broker of the Company in the 1730s, Laldas had to flee Surat and take refuge in the territory of the Peshwas. The dispute was engineered by his Parsi rivals.

More than anything else, it was overdependence on the agents that made the Company officers suffer from constant anxiety. The agent oppressed the subcontractors and weavers when he could, and defrauded the English whenever the opportune moment arose. Authorities in London warned the new recruit that, 'while he diligently performs his Duty . . . don't let him overtop you or be in effect Your Master'. And yet, there was little the headquarters in London could do to reform the system. Not only were the agents necessary, they were also at times supported by some of the English officers and the communities to which the brokers belonged. The feeling of powerlessness, then, expressed itself as abuses directed at an entire community. 'They are wealthy, subtle and malicious, as well as powerful; can bribe, devide, menace and by ill acts remove those that oppose them, being above shame and uncontroled by conscience', wrote a Surat officer in the late-1600s. The word 'dubash', literally bilingual, was rudely translated as two-faced by some of the European friends of the dubash.

None illustrates this complex relationship better than the one the Company had with Kasi Viranna, the leading dubash in Coromandel, referred to in the consultation books of 1661–90 as Verona. The Company could hardly move without his help in managing transport, procuring goods, loading goods, bringing back runaway boatmen, negotiating discounts on contracted prices and collecting taxes in Madras. Viranna was not a man of small means. His own ships plied between Madras and Bengal, which made him an especially useful procurement agent. And yet, the appointment letter of Streynsham Master, the chief of Coromandel, expressly urged him to avoid any situation wherein 'Verona, or any other one Man should be the Sole Merchant to Sell, buy and provide, for from thence many inconveniences may arise'. A similarly difficult relationship existed between the factors at Balasore and the chief broker in 1670, Chimchamshaw (Khem Chand Shah). The honesty of 'Chimcham' was not in doubt, but he was still found unreliable, because the poor man was squeezed between two masters, the Mughal governor who constantly harassed him for money, and the Company who found his loyalty questionable. In the early eighteenth century, the three sons of Rustam Manock, the leading Parsi house of Surat and rivals of Laldas, had a dispute with the Bombay Council who accused them of overcharging on a previous transaction. The strained relations continued until, upon an appeal from one of them who went to London for the purpose, the Court of Directors set up a special tribunal that settled in favour of the brothers.

Contracts with the weavers also suffered from the perennial suspicion of fraud. The system of buying cloth went through four stages in the entire period between 1620–1800. In the beginning, the Company simply bought cloth in the way it bought pepper in Southeast Asia, that is, from markets and bazaars. By the 1680s, contractual deals were made with a number of merchants who came to the factory with samples. The Masulipatnam consultations were written in this phase. In the early eighteenth century, the Company preferred to deal mainly with the chief brokers, or substantial merchants. After the Company became a ruler of Bengal, it tried to replace the independent merchant-contractors with paid employees. In this way, over time, the contractual ties between the trader and the producer strengthened in place of spot market purchases, and a more diverse group of middlemen got involved in the textile business.

Enforcement of contract was a serious problem. In the textile trade, delivery time was never predictable. Weavers routinely contracted with more buyers than they could supply to. Goods were diverted from contract sales to other bidders, from contract to spot markets, from the Company to private traders, and in Bengal, the Dutch and the English were played off against one another. The absence of a system of laws governing contractual sale made the Company overly dependent on the broker. And when the broker shifted the blame on the weaver for delays in delivery, the officers could only fret in impotent rage.

Private traders

The European private traders functioned in much the same way as the Company did, that is, they too hired agents. But they operated on a smaller scale than the chartered firms. And therefore, the relationship between the Europeans and the Indian agents worked rather more like a partnership than as an employer-employee one. As soon as he landed in Calcutta, the aspiring private trader would seek the help of friends in hiring 'writers' (clerks) and 'banyans' (agents). Those who arrived with substantial resources would be besieged by candidates for banyanship, 'quarreling like vultures for their prey', a Madras merchant explained. At the end of the eighteenth century in Bengal, it was usual for the writers to come from the Anglo-Indian society, and the banyan to be a Bengali. According to Stavorinus, the banyan's job was to 'note down all payments and receipts', and through his hands, 'all pecuniary matters go, as well as buying and selling'. They did not necessarily receive salaries, but 'they know how much more they may charge upon every rupee, than they have in reality paid.' Once again, suspicion of unfair prices was built into a relationship of dependence.

Contract

In the Company's correspondence, the business relation between Indians and Europeans were called 'contract' or 'compact' and some of the frictions that arose were called breach of contract. The word had no known Indian counterpart in the context of sale of goods. For all we know, the term was introduced in a one-sided manner by the Europeans. Clearly, this was so because large-scale purchase of any commodity on an advanced agreement by so large a firm was, if not an unknown form of exchange in India, certainly quite rare. It needed a new term.

The system of ordering and receiving cloth involved

elaborate written contracts between the chiefs of Bombay, Madras or Calcutta, and the merchants and master-weavers, specifying quantity, price, dimension, quality, advance payment and wages paid to the helping hands. When goods were delivered at the factory, senior officers examined the cargo and satisfied themselves that the terms of the contract had been fulfilled. In later years, 'contract' was extended to a wide variety of exchanges, for example, promises made by the Banjara caravan runners to supply grain to the Company's army. The insistence upon a written contract might seem surprising given that there was no law in India to deal with breach of contract. What good did a contract do then? In part, the contract made book-keeping easier. The head office in London did not trust its employees in India, and hence insisted on an unusual volume of paperwork. Moreover, the contract served as a binding moral obligation to some extent. Breaking a sale contract, if not exactly punishable under the Islamic law in force, was condemned as a sinful action.

In this way, a whole new world of business was created via the Company in the three port towns and the hinterland as well. Within India, the most far-reaching effect was seen in the unorthodox forms of business partnerships that this world made possible. Individuals without a family history of business entered business.

Indians joined Europeans in running firms. Eventually, such collaborations made these cities ideal sites for large-scale factories, which drew capital, enterprise and institutional support from many of the same groups who had been nurtured by Indo-European trade. Despite the advantages for both parties the principal-agent relations that developed around the Company were also fraught with discord and dispute. While it would be far-fetched to attribute the drive to colonize India to these discords, it cannot be denied that colonization did bring down the frequency of discords.

The immediate impetus to colonization, however, was the state of warfare in India.

A fleet of East Indiamen at sea, 1803, painting by Nicholas Pocock. A fleet returning from China, the group is dominated by the Hindostan, a large East Indiaman of 1248 tons, built in 1796. © National Maritime Museum, London.

WAR AND PLUNDER

IN 1707, EMPEROR Aurangzeb died. The vast empire the Mughals had ruled over for 180 years was on a decline and many provinces broke away to form independent states. Former provinces of the empire like Awadh, Hyderabad and Bengal became independent kingdoms, the Marathas based in western Maharashtra established dominions over Mughal provinces in Malwa, Berar and Bundelkhand and Rajput and Nayaka warlords consolidated their authority over smaller bits of territory in western and southern India.

This political turmoil was one of the factors for the emergence of English power in India. Both for safeguarding the Company's and their own interests as private traders, the Company employees began to take an active interest in Indian politics. Although initially they managed to maintain a distance from the turmoil, it was impossible for them to stay aloof for very long. In Bombay, there was a conflict with the Mughals over piracy in the 1690s. In Bengal, by the last years of Aurangzeb's reign, the Company had a considerable commercial stake, which led to disputes with the local authorities. The entry of the rival London Company occurred at the same time that Aurangzeb's grandson Azimusshan was appointed viceroy of Bengal. Azimusshan, a competent and successful military commander, first collected money from both the rivals and then decided that he could do better for himself by taking over the trading monopoly in Bengal. The English decide to tackle the threat by opening diplomatic relations with the Crown in Delhi and quietly arming themselves at the same time.

More than the external factors, it was the very functioning and structure of the Company in the eighteenth century that consolidated its political character. In their role as private traders, the employees interacted closely with local rulers, Indian merchants and landlords, often without the knowledge of the headquarters in London. Acquainted well with ground realities, these commercially ambitious employees had a deep understanding of local political situations. They had as allies the officers of the army that had been formed to guard the three territorial possessions of

Madras, Bombay and Kolkata. Alike in terms of social origin, these two groups shared similar ambitions and sometimes jointly planned undertakings to make money for the Company and for themselves. Many of their actions from 1746 onwards did not follow orders from the administrators in London.

This chapter describes the transformation of the Company into a war machine during that momentous time in Indian history, the eighteenth century.

The Carnatic affair

It was Anglo–French rivalry in the European theatre that upset what was until 1740 a barely stable equilibrium in India.

Of the major maritime nations in Western Europe, the French were the last to enter the race for India. One early initiative in 1604 came to nothing because of in-fighting. A second one in 1615 was too heavily dependent on Dutch sailors for its own good. In the next twenty years, a loosely organized effort to build a trading station in Madagascar did not yield any results. However, small settlements began in the islands of Mauritius, Reunion and Mascarenhas in the Indian Ocean. When La Compagnie des Indes was reconstituted in 1642, Madagascar was again a focal point as a possible base for a slave trade. But little was achieved except serious enmity with the inhabitants.

In 1661, Jean-Baptiste Colbert took over the reins of the French treasury. A merchant and banker by background, Colbert's priorities were the navy and overseas trade. A new company was formed in 1666, and the very next year the first mission to India set off. Certain events in the next five years led to strengthening of the French presence in India. Survivors of a bloody encounter in Madagascar in 1672 joined colleagues in India, bolstering the French manpower here. After trying to erect a fort in a number of places, from where the Dutch shooed them away, the French under François Martin (1634–1706) succeeded in building a fort in Pondicherry. In 1740, the French settlements in the Indian Ocean region consisted of the islands Pondicherry and Karaikal on the Coromandel, Mahé on the Malabar coast and Chandannagore in Bengal.

When hostilities broke out between the English and the French in Europe during the war of the Austrian succession, two French stalwarts dominated the politics in the Indian Ocean. In 1742, Joseph François Dupleix (1697–1763) was appointed the governor general of all French possessions in India. Marquis Dupleix, the scion of a landowning family, enlisted on a French Company ship when eighteen years old, built a large personal fortune, and briefly headed the mission in Bengal before taking over as the overall commander. What made him a special kind of leader was the ambition to establish French hegemony in Coromandel by military means. To this effect, he overhauled the army and looked for opportunities to form an alliance against the English. The other key individual was Bertrand-François Mahé de La Bourdonnais (1699–1753). Having distinguished himself as a naval officer in the employment of the French Company from 1718 to 1724, La Bourdonnais took up French government service and was deputed to the governorship of the islands in 1735.

These two lines, Dupleix and La Bourdonnais, joined in the Carnatic, a state located in the region presently bordering Tamil Nadu and Karnataka. In the previous sixty years, this region had been the theatre of a power struggle between the Telugu Nayakas, the states of Golkonda, Bijapur and the Marathas. Eventually a vassal of the Hyderabad state established a dynastic rule here. In 1740, a succession dispute broke out in the ruling family. The English in Madras and the French in Pondicherry were both worried about political instability in the region. Spurred by enmity in Europe, they took sides in the dispute and started a proxy war. Between 1746 and 1748, the British suffered reverses. They had to give up Madras and start a settlement in

Fort St David, a few miles to the south of Pondicherry. When peace was declared in Europe, and Madras was returned to the Company, the nervous leaders of Madras decided that their own well-being did not depend on following orders from London. Instead it lay in becoming a stronger military force. Robert Clive, a young clerk in Madras who had distinguished himself in the battles, soon had a voice in the push for autonomy.

In 1748, the palace dispute flared up again. The British sided with a claimant to the throne, Muhammad Ali, whereas the French backed Chanda Sahib, the rival. The Company gave shelter to the young prince in Madras, awarding an estate (jagir) for his upkeep. The jagir amounted to no more than two villages, but the gesture irritated the policymakers in London who wanted to keep out of local wrangling. Between 1749 and 1754, a series of disorderly battles were fought near Tiruchirappalli, with participation of European commanders and mercenaries on both sides. In these battles, which came to be known as the Second Carnatic Wars, the French side lost. Muhammad Ali, now with the additional title Walajah, assumed kingship of the Carnatic.

The Carnatic Wars had little effect on the political future of India, but it changed the character of the Company in Madras from a trading to a military entity.

Dupleix welcomed the shift, thinking that the Company was writing its own death warrant by committing itself to expensive deals at home and military adventures abroad. He told Ananda Ranga Pillai, 'The English Company is bound to die out. It has long been in an impecunious condition, and what it had to its credit has been lent to the King, whose overthrow is certain ... Mark my words.' Upon this calculation, Dupleix waited for the right moment to deliver the mortal blow. The third and final encounter between the English and the French erupted in the wake of the Seven Years War. Clive was one of the commanders on the English side. The French army was led by a royal officer Thomas Arthur, or Comte de Lally, the son of an Irish Jacobite and a French noblewoman. In the decisive encounter in Wandiwash in 1760, the French were defeated. Clive was now a kingmaker.

The negotiations leading up to the signing of the Treaty of Paris in 1763 became an occasion when disagreements between London and India came out in the open. The British government, for the first time, represented the East India Company to bring Indian territorial questions in a European forum. But it did not fully understand the clauses that Clive wanted to impose upon the French, which would guarantee an almost total French retreat in India. The directors of the

Company, represented by Laurence Sullivan, took a mediatory role. Their heart was with Clive, but their mind, guided as it was by mercantile considerations, dictated caution. In the end, Clive prevailed, but not before the relations between Clive and the Company had soured beyond repair. The treaty ensured that the French military power in India would be destroyed. The three heroes of the French political mission in India, La Bourdonnais, Dupleix and de Lally, faced severe criticism at home for adventures that had cost the treasury and the French Company an enormous sum of money. La Bourdonnais had already lost his property, was imprisoned, and died in poverty in 1753. Dupleix, who had staked his personal fortune on the Indian mission, went bankrupt and died unknown and poor in 1763. De Lally was executed in 1766.

In the Carnatic, the Company was a proxy for local dynastic struggles, whose outcomes were often unknown. The real test of Clive's generalship was Bengal, where the Company confronted a strong army.

Clive

Hailing from a minor gentry family of Shropshire overburdened with numerous children, Robert Clive (1725–74) grew up more or less away from home in the care of relatives and in boarding schools. As a young boy not known for his diligent scholarship, he had an adventurous and aggressive temperament. Having been trained in bookkeeping, a clerkship with the Company must have been a coveted and natural move. But the life of a ledger clerk in Madras bored him no end. Suffering from depression he attempted suicide but survived only because the pistol jammed. Amidst such gloominess, the Carnatic Wars came in as a breath of fresh air. When the wars ended, his superior, Stringer Lawrence, procured for him a commissariat job, which entailed a large private income for an entrepreneurial person. Clive built his fortune while still suffering from bouts of depression. In 1753, he married in Fort St David and returned with his wife to England. He had just settled down to the life of a politician when Clive was offered the position of governor of Fort St David.

Within months of his arrival, reports of a massacre of British officers and merchants of Calcutta reached Fort St David. Calcutta, it was reported, had been attacked by the nawab of Bengal, Siraj-ud-Daula, leading to a flight and genocide. How did things come to such a pass?

In Bengal, Aurangzeb's death had left little lasting political effect. One of his most efficient administrators, Murshid Quli Khan, continued to rule as the nawab, slowly breaking free from obligations to the court at Delhi. At Murshid Kuli's death in 1727, Bengal was nominally a Mughal province, but practically an independent state. Despite minor frictions, these events in Bengal politics did not trouble the English much. The nawabs were preoccupied. Murshid Kuli's main worry was the zamindars, who had grown too powerful during the collapse of the empire. His successors were harassed by Maratha raids. On their part, the English needed to keep leading courtiers in good humour because the Company could not get anywhere without the help of the nawab and his advisers. The system of currency and coinage, for example, was largely controlled by the firm of Jagatseth under state license; for any financial transaction the English necessarily had to appeal to him.

In the 1740s, the Maratha army of Berar attacked Bengal, seeking a share of the revenues. The nawab Alivardi Khan could do little to defend his territory from the repeated raids in western Bengal. When refused money by the king, the ill-disciplined mercenaries ransacked the villages, raided granaries and merchant homes, and abducted village women. The nightmarish memory of these raids still lives on in Bengali folklore. While these raids embarrassed the state and impoverished the people, Calcutta was growing in prosperity, population and military strength, very largely because of the raids. Unlike the other European factories that were located on the west bank of the river Hooghly, and therefore exposed to Maratha attacks, Calcutta was wisely situated on the east bank. In addition to the natural barrier of the river, the authorities dug a moat that they named Maratha Ditch. The moat was later filled to make for the Circular Road.

Calcutta in 1750 was not a pretty town. Swampy, dirty and disease-ridden, the city had a high death rate, so bad indeed that a Dutch visitor in the 1730s called it Golgotha. With all its ugliness, it was a haven of safety as well as a flourishing centre of trade. Between 1704 and 1756, the profit of the Company's estate in Calcutta had risen from less than Rs 500 to more than Rs 3000, the population of the city from 10,000 to 400,000, and the area of human settlement from eighty to 1600 acres. The rise in revenues from the markets enabled better policing of the city and measures to secure the defence in case of a Maratha attack. Attracted by the strong defence, a large number of Indian merchants, artisans and elite literate families resettled in Calcutta. It was not just a Company town any more; Calcutta was fast becoming the centre of Bengali enterprise and culture. The families of two illustrious Bengalis of late-eighteenth-century Calcutta, Nabakrishna Deb and Ramdulal Dey, were driven out of their ancestral homes in western Bengal by the Maratha raiders and took refuge in Calcutta in this time. In later life, Nabakrishna distinguished himself as an administrator under the English, and Ramdulal as a merchant. A number of other prominent Bengalis worked as administrators of the zamindari estate of Calcutta.

In this way, for some time, the nawab had been getting weaker and the Company stronger when the relationship soured rather suddenly in 1756. The bone of contention was the operation of English private traders in Bengal, who used the Company's license to refuse paying customs duty. The attack on Calcutta was the nawab's nervous remedy for the insolence of the English traders.

When Calcutta was attacked by Siraj-ud-Daula, many European residents of the city boarded the available boats and sailed away into safe distance, taking the cash boxes of the Company with them. But 146 English officers and a few women, many of them wounded, surrendered. In a sweltering night of June 1756, these prisoners were crammed into a dungeon 18-feet-square inside the Fort William. The room was walled on three sides and the remaining side was blocked by heavy iron bars. The prisoners offered huge bribes to the guards to be accommodated in two rooms. Mysteriously, the offer was rejected. When day came, more than a hundred were dead from suffocation, dehydration and trampling.

In the morning, the nawab received the news of the deaths with indifference, but flew into a rage on being told that the cash boxes were missing.

This incident was an important one in the history of India. Much like the Jallianwalla Bagh massacre 170 years later, it snapped a chord that had so far held a fragile relationship in delicate balance. Negotiation, which was the merchant's preferred method of dispute settlement, gave way to a desire for revenge. Conflicts so far had been a proxy war with the French; now for the first time a direct war with an Indian king was on the horizon.

Six months after Calcutta was lost, Clive and Vice-Admiral Charles Watson arrived at the mouth of the Hooghly with the entire forces of Madras, 1400 men in all. Watson and Clive did not particularly care for each other. Watson thought Clive was a scheming civilian masquerading as a soldier, and Clive thought Watson was an inept politician. Given their deep mutual dislike, it was a miracle how they managed to recapture Calcutta. For Watson the story was over with this victory. But Clive was in no mood to rest. He had guessed correctly that the young king's position was weak. With his impetuous behaviour, he had turned many friends into enemies, and was forsaken by his merchant allies and family elders. Through the mediation of prominent merchants, Clive opened secret negotiations with rivals to the throne.

The most powerful of these mediators was Amir Chand. At the time of these incidents, he was the largest of the Company's brokers in Bengal. Although a valuable ally, Amir Chand evoked much suspicion and wariness in the minds of his English friends. The night when Calcutta fell, he was already in prison, and Siraj-ud-Daula forgot to set him free. Some of the English officers who survived the dungeon deaths were told by the Indian guards that they were dumped in the 'black hole' under Amir Chand's secret instructions. He was, however, too powerful in the court to suffer on that account. In return for gathering the support of rival nobles, he demanded from Clive a 5 per cent cut on the treasure stored in the palace, 'or he would betray the whole design to the reigning nabob'. Not overburdened by ethics, and convinced that Amir Chand would double cross him, Clive drew up a false contract to secure the deal. After the Battle of Plassey, when Amir Chand was told that the contract was a forgery, he lost his mind.

Assured of support from nearly every potential claimant to the throne, merchants and key officers of the state, barring a few loyal military chiefs, Clive pressed on to the capital Murshidabad. In the Battle of Plassey on 13 June 1757, the nawab's forces fought a listless battle, surrounded by friends and relatives of the nawab who betrayed him.

When the victorious generals reached Murshidabad the next day, Siraj had left the city (to be caught and murdered a few days later). A court was summoned in the afternoon. Clive took Mir Jafar's hand and walked him to the throne, he then stood back and deeply bowed to the new nawab. These rituals over, the English officers went to inspect Siraj's treasury, and were rewarded with cash worth £2 million. Contemporary accounts state that the knowledge of a secret chamber in the nawab's inner quarters was carefully concealed from the English by four key Indian conspirators. When all was quiet, these four, including Mir Jafar and Nabakrishna Deb, visited the chamber and helped themselves to £8 million worth of pearls, jewels and gold coins. Over the next three years that he lived in India, Clive, now the Baron of Plassey, sent back several hundred thousand pounds in the form of bills drawn on the Dutch Company and Golconda diamonds.

There now began in the history of Bengal and the Company a sordid period that lasted almost twenty-five years. Bengal had effectively no ruler, because the English governed by proxy. Clive and his closest aide Henry Vansittart left the nawab in charge of the state while the Company was to defend Bengal on behalf of the nawab for a share of the revenue. English merchants fanned into the interior of Bengal. They used the Company's name to trade, evade duties and sometimes harass local people. The new nawab, an opium addict and respected by none, was happy with the arrangement. But some of his patrons were not. They feared that simply by doing nothing, he was losing the grip on the state finances on which the Company now depended so much.

In 1760, in a move that Vansittart proudly announced as a 'revolution', a rival noble Mir Qasim was installed as the king. Mir Qasim was a better administrator. But he also had ambitions. He wanted to raise the resources of the state, tax the English private traders, use the money to strengthen the state army and free himself of the odious dependence on the English. Vansittart was sympathetic to the king's drive to impose fiscal discipline. But others more mindful of the interests of the private traders wanted him out. One of the individuals who felt threatened by Mir Qasim's reforms was murdered in 1763, thrusting an unwanted war with the English on the nawab. In desperation, he sought the help of the tottering Muslim nobility of northern India, and found allies in the Mughal emperor Shah Alam II and the nawab of Awadh. All of them shared an anxiety about rising British power. But the armies that they got together proved to be a ragbag collection. Battles in Katwa, Giria,

Udhuanala (all in 1763) and Buxar (1764) were lost to disastrous decisions, divided command and desertion.

The thoroughly beaten Mughal emperor, in a face-saving gesture, gifted the charge of the revenues of Bengal, Bihar and Orissa to the Company against the payment of a tribute. Although the tribute was stopped ten years later, the aged emperor became a great friend of the Company. He began to admire many things European and lived under English protection.

Plunder

The key moment in the transformation of the Company from a trader to a sovereign had now arrived. It was 'invested now with full powers from the Mogul to act in a civil, military, and judicial capacity, without control' (Bartholomew Burgess, merchant, 1782). How did it use this power?

Soon after Plassey, state revenues were used to finance exports from India. Peasants were taxed and taxpayer's money was used to buy cloth for export. The availability of this option raised hopes among contemporaries of an end to silver import into India. H.V. Bowen has shown in a recent work that the hope was only partly fulfilled. The Company, from time to time, continued to bring in large quantities of silver long after 1760 and moved silver around between India and China more than before. Further, silver was also being imported by private traders, of which accurate estimates cannot be made. Ways to finance exports other than by silver, such as import of British goods and bills sold in India, were growing too. Nevertheless, the average import of silver did fall in the thirty years after the battle in Buxar.

Political power enabled the Company to address a problem that had plagued its business in India for a long time—poor contract enforcement. As the English settled in as rulers, a command-and-control system was devised to replace the unstable contracts which were in force. Brokers and agents were dispensed with. In Bengal and in Coromandel, the Company attempted to enforce closer control on the producers and appointed salaried officers to supervise contracts. These officials, armed with policing power, coerced the weavers to fulfill obligations and collected bribes and protection money right and left.

The wilderness continued in Bengal. Zamindars were rebellious, finances were in disarray, good administrators were in short supply and most Company officers, 'nabobs' as they were known, saw service in Bengal as an opportunity to get rich quick by milking the still rich treasury of the nawab. In London, the value of share of the Company crashed repeatedly, ruining many speculators, including some Parliamentarians. A violent famine in Bengal in 1770 exposed the indifference and incompetence of the state.

A short stint at leadership by Clive and his successor Harry Verelst saw only limited check on the rot. Verelst himself had owed his rise from a writer to a governor to private trade. The irony was not lost on other private traders. One of his many detractors, a former employee and merchant William Bolts, published a book attacking the corruption and chaos in Bengal. The book drew a rebuttal from Verelst. Back home in England, the two men continued to fight fruitless legal battles that bankrupted both of them. Both had assets in Bengal they were unable to recover. These exchanges brought about no great changes in Bengal itself, but drew public attention to the corruption that surrounded Company's rule in Bengal.

In one way, though, Verelst proved a visionary. He initiated the first formal discussion on how India should be ruled by Englishmen. He favoured indirect rule that would guarantee legal, social and cultural autonomy to the Indians, a principle that his more illustrious successor Warren Hastings (1732–1818) would enact into policy.

Hastings

Governor of Bengal (1772–73) and governor general of British India (1774–84), Hastings' leadership was significant for two important, though contradictory reasons. First, he instilled order in the administration and gave the Bengal government an institutional foundation. And second, through his own questionable conduct, he strengthened the lobby that favoured greater governmental regulation of India. Through these two ways, Hastings's tenure could be said to have ushered in imperialism in India.

Son of a clergyman and abandoned early by his father, Hastings was educated by his uncle at the Westminster School in London. His education was cut short by his uncle's death in 1750, so perforce Hastings had to take the job of a 'writer' of the Company. His first years in Bengal had formative effect on his personality. He learnt Persian from Nabakrishna. Being of the same age, the two men developed a close personal friendship. Hastings, therefore, attained maturity with a more intimate knowledge of the cultural and social life of the Indians than any other British officer in his milieu could claim to have.

Through the intrigue that led to the battle of Plassey, Hastings served in the army as a volunteer, and in 1758 was rewarded for his hard work with the senior position of resident at Murshidabad. While in Murshidabad, he sided with his friend Vansittart in supporting Mir Qasim. When Mir Qasim turned against his patrons, Hastings's life came in danger. For three days, as the nawab's men looked for him, he hid in a hut owned by a Bengali acquaintance, Kantobabu. In a dark room, Hastings survived on the diet of the poor Bengali, fermented rice and shrimp curry. He escaped unhurt, and so did Kantobabu. But the episode was a life-changing experience for Hastings. He became a blind believer in rewarding loyalty. And he developed a lifelong fondness for fermented rice and shrimp curry cooked in the rural Bengali style.

Immediately on returning to Calcutta, he faced the wrath of those colleagues who had opposed Vansittart's friendship with Mir Qasim. Having acquired neither money nor fame, he was sent back to England. In England, however, his public speeches on Indian affairs drew an interested audience. It was here that he outlined a future policy for India. The central tenet of the policy was that Bengal was a British province; that is, it could not be governed any more by the agents of the Company intent on making quick profits, and would need professional and experienced administrators. On the other hand, Bengal was also a complex entity with strong inherited cultural and administrative traditions.

Therefore, an effective British administration of the territory would need the officers to learn Persian, Sanskrit and Bengali, and rule by means of Indian traditional law.

In 1772, Hastings moved back to India and had the chance to implement his vision.

He took control of governance, reformed the administration of justice and the fiscal system. His judicial reforms incorporated the Indian legal systems that he had espoused earlier. His policy towards the local rulers in India was one of maintaining a peaceful distance, for which his cultural tolerance came in handy. He knew Persian well enough to hold conversations with Persian speakers without the aid of interpreters. With such accomplishments, it was no surprise that he was choosy about picking English officers. He dispensed with many whom he considered to be inexperienced, poorly trained, or driven by the prospect of personal gain, and replaced them with seasoned Indian hands. Hastings, in short, created a new model that could be called British India, one dominated by bureaucrats largely recruited from among the elites of India rather than merchants.

But he was also a failure on many levels mainly due to contradictions in his personality. While he wanted to rule justly, Hastings was also tolerant of his Indian protégés, the zamindars, turning a blind eye to the rampant exploitation and oppression they employed to raise revenues. Kantobabu, who had saved his life, was allowed to buy one zamindari after another using fraudulent means. Another loyal zamindar Devi Singh terrorized poor tenants, giving rise to peasant rebellion in Rangpur. Among lesser-known objects of Hastings' affection was one Jaffar, possibly a senior member of his personal guard, who had been presented with a large chunk of prime land near the Dharmatalla Street in Calcutta. Hastings' military campaigns led to much distress. In Benares, Rohilkhand and Awadh, the Company created dependencies against the promise of protecting them from Maratha raids. Peace reigned, but the Rohilkhand economy was in ruins, and the Awadh rulers lost any semblance of authority.

Hastings, finally, could do little to get rid of the factional fighting among members of the council of officers ruling Bengal, which escalated when the Parliament set up a Supreme Council to oversee the governor-general's work. The most formidable member of that body was Philip Francis, an able and knowledgeable writer on India who was secretly eyeing Hastings' job. The bad blood between the two men eventually claimed a high-profile Indian victim, Nandakumar.

Nandakumar was an officer in the nawab's service who had earlier served under Hastings. In 1775, he brought a public charge against Hastings of receiving bribe from the nawab. Had he won the case, Nandakumar could hope for rich rewards from Hastings's rivals, for he was almost certainly a protégé of Francis and an enemy of Hastings's old friend Nabakrishna Deb. However, events moved too quickly for him. A faction in the nawab's service loyal to Hastings brought a charge of forgery against Nandakumar in the newly established Supreme Court at Calcutta. The chief justice was Hastings's old school friend, Elijah Impey. Impey passed judgement on the case in a very short time and sentenced Nandakumar to death, a legitimate punishment for forgery in those days. No single episode hurt Hastings' reputation as badly as the death of Nandakumar. For the ordinary Bengalis it was symbolic of the amorality of the Company's rule, or 'European despotism' as an English merchant referred to it. The execution drew a massive crowd of spectators. As soon as it was over, thousands stampeded to the Hooghly to wash away the sin of watching the murder of a Brahman.

When Francis failed to gather enough support for his claim to the governor-general's seat, he collected a long list of complaints on corruption sponsored by Hastings. In 1785–86, these evidences found an enthusiastic and powerful audience.

Impeachment

Edmund Burke, philosopher, Parliamentarian, a leader of the Whig opposition and the most influential orator of his time, became interested in the Company possibly in the late 1760s, when the Parliament became worried about the fluctuating share prices. His own immediate family had suffered in the stockmarket crash. But Burke's misgivings about the Company were founded not only on personal experience. In the 1770s, he was appointed a member of a select committee assessing a 1773 regulating act. Once his gaze was fixed upon India, one example after another of high-handed actions by Company officers seemed to present themselves.

In the next ten years, Burke developed a precise critique of Company rule in India. For him, a rule by merchants seeking profits, in a world where institutions of the state were lacking or had been destroyed, created untrammelled corruption everywhere. This was true of course. But his views about the Company government still needed a point of reference, and here Burke's ignorance about India was exposed. Many of the acts of corruption he accused the Company of, the employees of the Company believed were part of the Indian tradition of statecraft, the practice of obligatory cash rewards or bribes to officers of state, for example. In Burke's mind, the proxy wars in the Carnatic were acts of political cynicism. In fact, in eighteenth-century India, military and political opportunism was the norm, not an exception introduced by the British.

Having identified a whole system gone wrong, Burke pounced on a single individual in his search for a remedy. Harnessing all of his extraordinary intellectual and moral energy, he fell upon Hastings. Francis eagerly supplied him classified information on Hastings. One man now epitomized the whole rotten system in India. A highly charged Burke persuaded the Parliament to launch an impeachment, or a trial before the Lords, against Hastings. The trial began in 1788, three years after Hastings had returned home, intending to spend the rest of his life as a country squire.

There was every sign that Hastings enjoyed the public attention at first, partly because he was convinced that there was no case against him, and partly for the reason that the trial was a crowd-puller. However, Burke's formidable oratory, the mounting cost of the trial, and the dirty linen that came to be washed in public eye, made this a serious business for him. Among the charges against him were those of taking bribes, the death sentence of Nandakumar and sheltering cruel and corrupt zamindars as a reward for personal loyalty.

Serious as these charges were, the nine-year long trial ended with an overwhelming verdict of not guilty, to general public approval. Burke had overstepped judicial propriety by accusing Hastings of conspiring to murder Nandakumar. The more serious charges of personal corruption could not be proven, and it looked to almost everyone except Burke that Hastings was being made something of a scapegoat. Burke lost the case, but the significance of the point he made was not lost on the Parliament. Governance in India could not be left to the discretion of a group of opportunistic men driven by the lure of making quick money. With this episode, it can be said, the British empire in India began.

Burke drew inspiration from a book published six years before the trial began, a book that had already done irreparable damage to the case for the Company.

Adam Smith

In 1776, Adam Smith published *An Inquiry into the Nature and Causes of the Wealth of Nations*. The book presented a case for liberalism. For this purpose, it was necessary to destroy the case for monopoly. Smith's primary example of the abuses of monopoly was the East India Company. But unlike contemporary critics of monopoly, who had confined themselves to the damage that monopoly caused to private enterprise, Smith also considered the economy of Bengal. The Company in India, for him, was an example of a special kind of distortion. Monopoly was bad, but far worse was a monopolist that ran a state. Having shown how the monopoly charter had led to an inflation of Indian goods in British markets, Smith argued that a government run by traders made private profits rather than public welfare the goal of the state, and hurt commerce itself. 'If the trading spirit of the English East India Company', he wrote, 'renders them very bad sovereigns; the spirit of sovereignty seems to have rendered them equally bad traders'. Having become preoccupied with warfare and political contest, the Company exposed itself to bankruptcy and ever more dependence on government support.

Justly influential as this assessment was, Smith was not completely correct in his evaluation of the situation in India. He assumed that the countries such as Bengal where the Europeans ruled were 'more fertile, more extensive; and, in proportion to their extent, much richer and more populous than Great Britain'; which led him to conclude that European plunder reduced a wealthy people to poverty. The truth was that Bengal was a considerably poorer region than England in the 1770s. Plunder, a favourite word in Smith's vocabulary apropos the non-Western world, was directed at the jewel hoards of the idle rich in India rather than the savings of the ordinary folk. Further, in his attempt to prove his assumptions right, Smith overlooked the organizational character of the Company. He did not see the split personality of the firm. What he saw happening in India was not, as he believed, a move orchestrated by the London merchants pursuing the path of an expansionist monopoly, but one pushed by the traders and soldiers stationed in India against the advice of the stakeholders in London. Contrary to his analysis, the conquest of Bengal was a sign of weakness of the firm, not a sign of its strength.

Still, Smith gave a theoretical shape to a historic misgiving on monopoly. He placed Indian interests squarely in the middle of the debate on the East India Company. And he drew attention to the real danger posed by a coincidence between profit-seeking and running a state.

Regulating Act

The apparatus for control and regulation of the Company's territories by the Parliament had already been in the making.

The decade following the Company's elevation as the revenue administrator of Bengal caused much embarrassment to the government in Britain. The Company's representatives in India worked in open defiance of orders from above. Some who had gone to India as clerks or lieutenants returned home with diamonds and gold presented to them by grateful Indian princes. The Bolts-versus-Verelst affair was a scandal. The territorial acquisitions raised a question of principle. Who did these lands belong to, the Company or the Crown?

The Company itself was in a crisis as its military enterprise cost huge amounts of money, the textile business was in trouble because of the rising prices of cloth in India, and income from tea fell because of new taxes. The revenues from Bengal, for some time used to finance trade, war and the establishment, did not increase as much as was necessary, and in fact suffered a shock after the 1770 famine in Bengal. The stockmarket reflected these uncertainties, on several occasions bringing the Company to the brink of disaster. In short, the nabobs seemed to have ruined the employer that they worked for.

The Company as ruler in India posed an awkward problem in British politics. Could there be two sovereigns ruling in the name of Britain, or should all overseas empires belong to the one and only Crown? The king himself, George III, had enough distractions at home to be interested in the kingship of Bengal. The Company maintained the pretence of ruling in the name of the king. But the rule was founded on principles of profit, which, many believed, had delivered a corrupt rule for the Indians in the name of the king of Britain. Popular support for political missions in the East was quite low in view of the fluctuations in the share market. All of this provided ammunition to the faction of the Parliament seeking more regulation of the Company.

In 1772, the prime minister Lord North approved a large loan towards a rescue operation, together with reformed taxation on tea that fuelled the demand for independence in America. North was one of those politicians who believed that the Company's acquisitions in India ought to be governed by the Crown. If he desisted from carrying out this agenda, it was because the Company's role was already in the process of getting regulated. An East India Regulating Act in 1773 raised the salaries of the Indian administrators while prohibiting them from private trade. The Act also provided for a Supreme Court for Calcutta. North's Regulating Act, by imposing the Parliament's authority upon European settlers in India, consolidated the empire in Asia. Interestingly, the same movement unleashed forces that led to the unmaking of another empire in North America. As the historian Peter Marshall has shown in a recent book, quite in contrast with the situation in India, the American settlers, believing that they were

British subjects born to liberty, fiercely resisted colonial authority.

Within India, efforts to bring comprehensive legislation matured in 1784, when a Parliamentary Act brought about by William Pitt established a more or less permanent framework for the administration of the Company's territories in India. The Act subordinated the political affairs of the Company to a regulatory body set up by the Crown, known as the Board of Control. The demarcation of politics and economics, Crown and the Company, remained unclear for a long time afterwards. But the question, who really ruled India, became steadily less relevant with the increasing autonomy of the office of the governor general in India.

By the turn of the nineteenth century the East India Company had been transformed from a trader to an empire-builder. A new breed of aggressively imperialist heads of state, backed up by the Parliament, completed the transition.

'The Political-Banditti Assailing the Saviour of India', 1786. Warren Hastings, dressed like a Turkish general, rides a camel laden with the Company's hard-earned money. He is attacked by Edmund Burke (left), Frederick, Lord North (centre) and Charles James Fox (right). © British Library Board.

RULER IN INDIA

THE FIRST STEPS in the direction of an empire began in Bombay. Frequent skirmishes with the Marathas and periodic run-ins with the smaller states of Gujarat led the Bombay Presidency to a fiscal crisis in the last decades of the eighteenth century. The administration considered winding up Bombay, but desisted on being persuaded by the private traders that the port still had life left in it, provided the Company could befriend and subdue the many kings who ruled the coast. The result was an alliance with Malabar and minor conquests in Gujarat and Saurashtra. The beginning of an opium trade with China brightened the prospects of the port city further. By the time of the Napoleonic wars, when cotton exports boomed, Bombay was firmly back in business.

The Napoleonic wars rekindled Anglo-French rivalry. During the Mysore Wars with Tipu Sultan, and the Second Anglo–Maratha War in 1803, the Indian armies were led by French generals. The French were subdued, but the scene was set for a decisive showdown with the only remaining Indian military rival, the Marathas. When the Third Anglo-Maratha War ended in 1818, the Company was effectively the ruler of India.

To the contemporaries, the Company dominions were a different kind of state from the Indian ones. Despite the failure of Hastings to take firm command of the zamindars, his successors managed to impose their writ on the local bosses and thus controlled the fiscal and the military machine with a firm hand. Unlike most Indian states that relied on soldiers supplied by warlords and noblemen, the Company had a standing army financed out of expanding credit and land revenue. The government was run by administrators and not by bejewelled noblemen. Sensing the advantage, the governor Richard Wellesley (in office: 1796–1805) pursued a policy of imperialist expansion.

Commercial leadership, as this chapter will show, was passing on to private hands. Curiously, many amongst these private capitalists had become prosperous under implicit patronage of the East India Company.

The end of Company trade

The Company's business had undergone a monumental change between 1750 and 1810. By the second half of the eighteenth century, China became a very important growth area for the Company's business. Initially the interest in the tea trade was secondary to textiles. But partly in response to massive growth in demand, which the private traders made the most of, and partly because of a Parliamentary prohibition of import of finished textiles (1720), tea emerged as the main business of the Company. As long as both Indian cloth and Chinese tea were paid for with silver acquired in Spain, India and China trades did not directly interact. But when silver flows became uncertain during the war of American independence, the Company needed to find ways of paying for tea with Indian goods. From the end of the eighteenth century, as we see below, Indian opium provided an answer to this need.

Involved as it had become with local affairs, the Company also lost much ground as a trader in India. Its textile business had been stagnant in volume for a long time, and began to decline after 1800 as the Industrial Revolution gained momentum. 'Before the profitable trade of war . . . gave a mortal check to honest industry, the loom furnished a great and flourishing commerce', wrote the Welsh naturalist Thomas Pennant in 1798. The 'mortal check' did not come from the 'profitable trade of war', however. The more serious check came from the invention and rapid spread of machine-spinning of yarn. A reverse flow of yarn into India began from the early 1820s and cloth soon followed, finally ending a 200-year trade in Indian textiles.

On Indian shores, the Napoleonic wars left the fledgling American merchant fleet in a position of unusual strength. It was the only neutral shipping in the world's waters. After the French and the Dutch East India Companies were disbanded at the end of the wars, and the English Company struggled on militarily and financially, the Americans occupied the premier place as the world's carriers of Asian goods.

The retreat of the Company from trade opened the gates to economic migrants of many kinds. By 1800, Madras, Bombay, and especially Calcutta, had become home to substantial communities of Europeans and Indians who had adopted European habits. In the preceding decades, warfare had given rise to a military labour market in which Europeans commanded high wages. European mercenaries offered their services to the Maratha generals of Bundelkhand and Malwa, to Ranjit Singh of Punjab, Tipu Sultan in Mysore, and many others besides. The growing population of Europeans and the high wages that some of them received had stimulated demand for European-style consumer goods in India. Settlers created a market for carriages, furniture, palanquins, crockery and cutlery, saddles, boots and shoes, salted meats, guns and pistols, watches and silverware. While some of the goods were imported, many immigrant European and Indo-European artisans made these goods in the Indian port cities.

A remarkable set of people who came to India in this time were the so-called Company painters. Some of them were contracted to paint Indian scenes for the edification of the officers, and others were fortune-hunters who hoped to create a market for their goods in Britain. Seen against Indian painting traditions, these artists developed a new idiom steeped in a historic-romantic mood. A good example of the difference between the old and the new styles of landscape painting would be the pictures of nawabi Murshidabad painted after 1757. A court artist painted the town as a joyous fairground where Hindus and Muslims, the poor and the rich, kings and commoners, men and women, met to have a good time together. Charles D'Oyly's paintings of the town showed the desolate ruins of the magnificent Katara Masjid against the fading lights of a setting sun.

1813: End of monopoly

At the end of the 1700s, a number of English merchants and firms were doing business in the Company's government. Often in partnership with Indians, they set up import-export businesses in Calcutta. Dependent on the Company for trading licenses and repatriation of profits, they resented the dependence too, and campaigned for its end in Britain. They wanted the empire the Company had created, but did not necessarily want the Company to run a business using this power. The unfolding battle had much to do with the transformation of business in Britain.

For some time, there had been a growing rift between the group that two historians Peter Cain and Anthony Hopkins call 'gentlemanly capitalists', that is, bankers-cum-politicians centred in the City of London, and the manufacturers spread in the provincial towns. The former group was politically close to the owners of the Company, and had increased in wealth and power during the Napoleonic wars, which made London the global banking capital over Amsterdam and other continental financial centres. At the same time, a different class of capitalists, the merchants of the English provincial towns, was leading the Industrial Revolution. The Indo-European firms were, socially speaking, closer to this group, and shared more economic interests with them. When the Company's charter came up for renewal in 1793, only a modest concession was made to them, since the resistance of London merchants to a dilution of the charter was still quite strong. The new charter allowed for a part of the Company's fleets to be used by private merchants. But this concession did not amount to much. Private merchants complained of the high freight rates and did not want to be tied to the Company's warehouses.

These firms imported food and raw material from America. Wars in Europe and with America disrupted the trade, and increased the importance of India as an alternative source of raw material. These people were not the political mainstream, but inflation in food prices turned the balance of political advantage in their favour. Rising prices of bread led to import of rice from India and fears of possible shortage of American cotton saw efforts to import Indian cotton. The Company, as a conciliatory move to the manufacturing groups, had begun importing cotton from India. But the Liverpool merchants were not happy with the quality of Indian cotton, and argued argued reasonably that the end of the monopoly would see more cotton traders going to India to influence the peasants' cultivation methods. The demands were relayed by Indian administrators to the commission of enquiry deciding the renewal of the Company's charter in 1812–13.

Although the wars consolidated the power of the gentlemanly capitalists, in 1813, the City of London was still in turmoil, unable to act in concert, and was losing interest in commodity trade. The manufacturers and petty traders, therefore, won the battle for the end of the charter, as Anthony Webster's recent work has shown. In 1813, the new charter ended the Company's monopoly of Indian trade. The Company did not cease to trade in India. It continued to import some silk and indigo thereafter. But the scale was smaller, and it began to wind up its factories one by one. The monopoly in the China trade was retained, and the freedom offered to private trade in India was restricted to the main Company settlements. Nevertheless, the concessions granted to provincial capitalists were unprecedented.

Agency houses

The practice of Company employees trading on their own was prohibited in the 1780s, opening up a vast field of enterprise for London merchants and participants in country trade to join in. With a new sense of empowerment egging them on, European private traders moved further inland. A new business, indigo manufacturing, became a field of employment of European capital. The production side of the business was located in the Bengal and Bihar countryside, often days' journey away from Calcutta. The marketing and the financial arms were based in Calcutta. 'Houses of agency' in Calcutta supplied credit to the planters, acted as agents of these firms, and handled remittances of profit.

Until 1813, the relationship between these firms and the Company was a bundle of contradictions. There was close interdependence. The Company's bill of exchange, for example, was a favourite mode of remittance for the agency houses. Individuals moved between private enterprise and Company service with facility. The conquest of India had taken place in the teeth of opposition from the Company administrators in London. Standing up for private enterprise and expansion of British dominion were some individuals who had made their wealth in India. For example, David Scott of Bombay and Charles Cockerell of Calcutta, who had made their fortunes in the agency business, spent a great deal of their savings in supporting the growth of the empire in India. Still, the private interests of these firms frequently led them into quarrels with the Company. They did not like the Company in its role as a regulator of trade. Charles Forbes, one of the founders of the Bombay firm Forbes, Forbes and Campbell, spent the better part of his career as a politician in Britain campaigning against the monopoly charter.

Three examples illustrate the early history of these

first multinationals especially well. The founder of Paxton, Cockerell, & Co. was William Paxton, a soldier and mariner in his youth. In later life he joined the Company's service as an assayer of gold and silver. While in this job, he started out as a trader in partnership with a colleague, Charles Cockerell. Both men made their money in India and culminated their careers as prominent merchant-bankers in London. Paxton was the great-grandfather of Archibald Wavell, one of the last viceroys of India. Palmer & Co., the largest of the agency houses about 1830, was established by a son of William Palmer, a Company officer and contemporary of Hastings. Palmer & Co. was a partnership between the brothers George and John Horsley Palmer. Although the Calcutta firm failed in 1833, the London end of the business survived and George Palmer later became a governor of the Bank of England. In 1813, Kirkman Finlay, son of James Finlay, managed an expanding empire of trade from his base in Glasgow. The firm of James Finlay was a leading cotton trader of Bombay in the 1870s and ended the nineteenth century as the major plantation company of south India.

In the middle of the nineteenth century, a new wave of entry into the world of Asian trade took place. Many of the firms that were then established, such as Mackinnon-Mackenzie, Jardine-Matheson and David

Sassoon, had presence simultaneously in Bombay, Calcutta, Singapore and Hong Kong, and were beginning to diversify from indigo and opium into steam navigation, tea plantations, breweries, tramways, construction and textile mills. They were a product of the time when the British empire was already an accomplished fact.

In all three cities, the agency houses developed close ties with Indian merchants and entrepreneurs. In Bombay, Jamsetjee Jeejeebhoy formed a partnership with Charles Forbes, and was the chief agent of Jardine-Matheson, the agency house of Canton. In Calcutta, between 1833 and 1846 Dwarkanath Tagore, the most prominent Bengali entrepreneur of his times, was a partner of William Carr and William Prinsep. A number of lesser known Indian firms and individuals partnered with European enterprise in indigo and opium.

It was not only merchants who came to India after 1813, many artisan-entrepreneurs did too. Tanneries, glass works, iron smelting and carpentry workshops were established. In Calcutta, Madras and Bombay could be found 'British artisans and manufacturers of almost every description of trade that is exercised in [Britain]'. The area within these cities, which were to develop factories after 1850, began to grow as hubs of artisan enterprise. A good example would be the river bank across Calcutta, in Howrah, where shipyards and warehouses had begun to develop long before the jute mills and engineering factories of the late nineteenth century.

Opium trade and China: 1813–33

A major interest of the agency houses was export of Bihar opium to China. The opium was made under license from the Company, but it was transported and sold in China by European and Indian firms who owned specially designed ships known as opium runners. The opium was paid for with the Company's bills on India or London. The sellers either drew bills against silver, or paid for opium in the first instance with silver, which was exchanged for bills. By drawing bills in Canton, the merchants could safely remit their money to Bombay or London, whereas the Company received the silver that it needed to buy Chinese tea. In this way, opium enabled the Company to partially meet its adverse trade balance with China.

The rates of exchange at Canton were favourable enough to make this form of transfer cheaper than sending goods. The Company's sponsorship enabled the Indian and European merchants to deal with their counterparts, a group of Hong merchants who, 'with unity and vigour', maintained control on the officially outlawed trade. The Hong network helped the Company's servants and private merchants to protect the opium runners from pirate attacks. Pirates, in turn, were interested in these ships for the silver that they often carried.

The private merchants were not necessarily happy about the complex arrangement. They were technically hired on contract, or agency. That is, they were licensed to trade only between India and China, and the license barred them from trading with Britain. Chinese official injunctions against the Company exposed the private traders to the risk of confiscation and harassment. Steadily after 1813, therefore, the major firms that dominated the China trade grew less dependent on the Company's protection and began to push for an end to the Company's monopoly of the China trade, which finally happened in 1833.

The final years

From 1833, the Company ceased to exist as a trading body. It existed as an administrator of India in partnership with the Crown. The partnership was an unequal one. The Company's own Court of Directors still had some say in Indian affairs, but the Board of Control, in which the government dominated, had far more say in matters of policy. Nevertheless, the Company's symbolic authority was still recognized in Britain and in India. In Britain, it was acknowledged by business and political leaders that the Company, in making an Indian empire possible, had performed a historic role in the remarkable growth of Britain's own industrialization. This was affirmed by the emphatically positive vote with which the Parliament endorsed the formal right of the Company to administer India in 1853.

Shortly after the regulating acts were installed, debates and discussions about how to govern India began in earnest. Much research has taken place, and is still taking place, on the Company as a government. Recent writings on the theme—by Sudipta Sen and Philip Stern for example—explore the early 'discourse' on trade policy and regulation. Others, such as David Washbrook, have studied law and administration. Without going into this vast scholarship here, it is possible to say that a build-up of infrastructure and institutions enabled the Company to integrate a politically fragmented region into one vast country.

Between 1780 and 1850, for example, the Company set up the most powerful standing army the region had seen, established courts of law and gradually turned its attention away from conquest to governance. Conquest did not stop, but except the wars in Punjab, was achieved by bloodless means. Significant steps were taken towards canal construction in south India, the building of the railways, the telegraph, and universities. The Industrial Revolution had made India a potentially valuable source of food and raw material. Cotton was already being exported from Bombay to Lancashire in large quantities. If this report card suggests a rapid modernization, the impression is a misleading one. With respect to Indian society, the British administration in India continued to tread cautiously. It had instituted new courts of law, but filled the law books with Indian religious codes. Where possible, it had granted land rights to established peasant clans and landlords. Much of the new infrastructure—the railways, canals, telegraph, and universities—came in late in the 1850s, and represented a new viceroy's particular vision of India.

Against the backdrop of peaceful inactivity, the mutiny came as a shattering blow. An event that unleashed fury against the British on an unimaginable scale, it caught the rulers of India unprepared. Suddenly the Company was again in the line of fire. Even though the Parliament had acted in concert with every major administrative decision since 1788, the Company was more exposed to public scrutiny than was the Board of Control. When, in December 1857, the government gave a hint that the

Indian empire would henceforth be administered by the Crown, the Company hurriedly commissioned its most able employee, the great libertarian philosopher and economic theorist John Stuart Mill, to write a petition in its defence to be submitted to the Parliament.

Mill's report was the finest requiem the Company could get. Mill made the case that the Company in 1855 was a far cry from the days of monopoly and corruption. It had won Britain an empire in India, when the Crown had lost one in America. By running a government that left Indian institutions intact and refusing to install British political systems and ideas, the Company provided the most pragmatic form of governance in India. It was the result of an accident of history no doubt, but one that had turned out well, and did not deserve to be replaced. Mill's petition failed, not least because such arguments, all of them partly valid, could not explain the mutiny.

On 1 September 1858, the Court of Directors met for the last time in their office in Leadenhall Street, and voted unanimously to pass the only item on the agenda, grant of an annuity for John Lawrence, the lieutenant-governor of Punjab, who had played a stellar role in suppressing the mutiny in north India. Exactly two months later came the Queen's pronouncement declaring British India a Crown possession. By a stroke

of the pen, the administration and the army, hitherto in
the employment of the East India Company, transferred
to the service of British India. Long before that date, the
Company as a business had come to an end.

Playing chess. Painting by Charles Gold, 1791. A rare picture of a social moment shared equally.
© British Library Board

THE COMPANY AND
INDIAN HISTORY

THE SIGNIFICANCE OF the East India Company for British economic transition has been the subject of a long-running and lively debate. Its significance for the Indian economic transition in the period 1600-1857 has received less attention. The final chapter of the book rethinks this issue.

It is useful to divide the subject into three parts, effect on business organization; the effect of the Company's trading operations on economic change in India; and the role of the Company government in shaping economic growth or stagnation.

Business organization

The effect of the Company on business organization in India is an under-researched subject. Still, two positions can be distinguished. One of these suggests that by representing rational, forward-looking, productivity-oriented firms, the English and the Dutch ushered in a commercial revolution. They were simply more efficient than the conservative and traditional Indians or the aggressive Portuguese traders. Critics of this view point out that the companies were so heavily dependent on Indian agents, and consequently on customs and institutions already present in the region, that European success cannot be understood with reference to European business organization alone. They advance the alternative view that the task requires a consideration of the highly developed business organizations already in existence in India.

There are problems with both these positions. The former view underestimates the difficulties the companies faced in India and the adaptations and compromises that they had to make. The latter does not allow us to see any institutional effect of European trade at all. In fact, the European and the Indian worlds of business were indeed quite different, and both were affected by the close contact. The outcome of the meeting between these two worlds was not the triumph of one over the other, but the creation of new rules for the game. These new rules enabled trade, but also gave rise to frictions, disputes and unintended results.

The main point of difference between the Europeans—what is said below of the English should apply equally well to the Dutch as well—and the Indians was not one of efficiency, but one of scale. The success of private trade showed that the monopoly firm was not a very efficient business model in the 1700s. And yet, the joint-stock form and the monopoly charter made a major qualitative difference in a world where family- and community-run businesses still ruled supreme. It allowed the Company to operate on a scale of business that was infinitely larger than what the Indian firms would manage on average. The enormously large scale, and the large capital that the Company utilized in India, had no Indian counterpart because the notion of joint stock did not have an Indian precedence.

An unintended result of the huge scale was the extensive use of contractual purchases. This was the real innovation the Company introduced in India, the idea and the practice of contract. Contractual transactions were not unknown in India. Some textile business in domestic overland trade was conducted under contract, though exactly under what terms and conditions remains unknown. Both the Hindu dharmashastras and the Islamic codes dealt with the subject of contract, as the early colonial legislators discovered. But they also discovered that such codes were not much used in practice, and the effort to make use of religious codes on contract in settling actual trade disputes in the British Indian courts ended in a complete failure. The Indian merchants never expressed a preference for their own religious contract laws. This is not surprising. The association with religion would have made these codes too sectarian to be practically useful, and the codes covered debts better than sales. Be that as it may, contracts on the scale and complexity that the Europeans introduced, involving so many subcontractors and such long delivery time, did not have an Indian precedence. In turn, the difference owed to the very large scale of operations that the company form made possible.

In the beginning, the Company procured what cloth or pepper it could get from local merchants. Spot market sale rather than contractual sale was the norm. Increasingly, it engaged brokers, headmen and contractors to procure goods on long-period contract. Orders involved millions of yards of cloth at a time and involved hundreds of villages. Orders were placed and secured by paying millions of pounds in ready cash more than a year in advance. All of this was backed by the contract form the parties signed on. The documents registered advances paid and specified the quality, design, price and quantity of the goods in detail. Quality specifications, needless to say, were of critical importance when the goods in question were fashionable textiles.

All contracts work on the basis of trust. Somebody advances money. Others promise to deliver a good or a service on time and of required quality. In the absence of a court settling contractual disputes, how would any party ensure that promises would be kept? Indians ensured that promises would be adhered to by confining the most consequential exchanges—credit, land, or knowledge—within the community, and by making the whole community responsible for honest conduct. The Europeans did not have access to either community resources or courts of law in their operations in India. Therefore, principal-agent relations were fraught with problems. Weavers took advances and ran away or short-changed on quality, brokers took bribes from everybody, and agents took advantage of the rivalry between the Dutch and the English and the tensions between the nawab and the Company. Frictions of such kinds formed the staple subject of official correspondence, and showed up in the invectives that the Europeans routinely directed at their closest allies, the 'Bania'.

The possibility of contract failures was not necessarily bad news for the Indians who had dealings with the Company. Precisely because there was such a possibility, those agents and partners deemed trustworthy were rewarded not only in money but also in status, patronage and power. By 1750, the results of trust and reward could be seen in the three cities where the Company had established mini-states with its own laws.

The rapid growth of commerce and industry in these three cities owed to a form of Indo-European enterprise that was different from anything that the traditional Indian business system could offer. These cities made the world economy more accessible to the Indians. They reduced the weight of caste and community and made unorthodox alliances possible. The cities, therefore, allowed Indians who had no past exposure to trade to participate in commercial enterprise internationally. They created a freer society where interactions between ethnic groups were considerably easier than in the interiors of India. They introduced cosmopolitanism, the hallmark of urban modernity.

Trade and economic change

Although as a firm it overshadowed all others, how large was the Company in relation to commerce as a whole?

In the backdrop of the Indian economy as a whole, the European companies taken together were far too small a player to make any difference, good or bad, directly through trade. Their scale of trading operation was tiny when measured against the size of the economy.

The proportion of textile export to the production of textiles has been variously measured. The most generous measure is 10 per cent for Bengal about 1750. My own figure for the share of export in total production of cotton cloth in the Indian subcontinent is 1–2 per cent in 1795. Cloth itself could not have had more than a 10 per cent share in the domestic product. We are then talking about a form of economic activity which did not occupy more than a thousandth part of the economy. The English Company's own share in that slice of business was about two-thirds. Realizing how small this trade was should quickly settle some unnecessary debates. For example, some historians puzzle over the fact that the 'large' inflow of silver did not have much effect on Indian prices, as they did in contemporary Europe. They have attributed this inertia to the fact that the Indians converted a lot of the silver into ornaments rather than coins. It would be simpler to note that the silver inflow was too small in the first place.

If Indo-European trade has received so much attention from historians it is a reflection not of their true scale relative to the Indian economy, but the infinitely richer archival records available on overseas trade, compared with an almost barrenness of data regarding domestic trade. The officers of the English company produced a mountain of records and retained much of it because they worked for a joint-stock company. They had to explain things to their employers, shareholders, the Parliament and the Crown. The Indian firms wrote their accounts in archaic, mysterious language, fudged the numbers deliberately, and then held these papers close to their chest because these were family heirloom and no business of anyone. A usual lament of the doctoral student in history is the scarcity of business papers of old Indian firms. It is likely that the scarcity does not reflect a scarcity of records as such, but also the persistence of the sentiment that long considered these records a private asset.

Having said that, we would be quite wrong to conclude that Indo-European trade was an illusion sustained by records. It is of course true, as the historian Sushil Chaudhury reminds us, that the significance of overland and domestic trade remains underestimated. But it is also true that the significance of overseas trade cannot really be grasped merely in quantitative terms. Its real importance lay in its impact on business organization, and in this respect, overseas trade had a far deeper and lasting effect than domestic and overland trades. The point needs labouring, because of its implication for political change. The drive to colonize India cannot be understood with reference to how big the business of foreign merchants was; we need to consider instead how easy or difficult it was to build productive partnerships between the Indians and the Europeans. And I have suggested above that, though large in scale, it was a difficult partnership.

In a more obvious sense, Indo-European trade was undoubtedly important to India. Trade was the handmaiden of empire.

State and economic development

If the effects of the Company on Indian business has remained under-researched, the effects of the early empire on prospects of economic development has become too politicized a subject to lend itself to a dispassionate discussion. The default view, which was engraved in the collective consciousness of the Indians by the nationalist writers, started from the assumption that India had been a prosperous place to begin with. The kings and the nawabs had set up a haven of welfare and enterprise in their domains. The Company defeated these good kings by treachery, and then set out to extract Indian wealth in order to enrich Britain. The money looted and sent home or the tax revenue used for the purpose of trade in the last quarter of the eighteenth century was a politically engineered 'drain' of Indian resources. Indians were made poor by these exploitative but powerful foreign merchants, according to the 'drain theory' of Indian poverty.

No doubt the early Company fiscal policy was based on corrupt practices. The allegation of corruption was made back in the 1770s, in the wake of the battle between the supporters of the Company and the anti-monopoly lobby in the British Parliament. Many of the facts cited in present-day history were first employed to make a case for government regulation of Indian administration in the 1770s. Precisely because the whole discourse was political in nature, we need to be careful with recycling the arguments of Edmund Burke, Adam Smith and other contemporary critics.

It is difficult to build a 'theory' of Indian poverty on the basis of the corruption of early Company rule. Much of the money that Clive and his henchmen looted from India came from the treasury of the nawab. The Indian princes, 'walking jeweller's shops' as an American merchant called them, spent more money on pearls and diamonds than on infrastructural development or welfare measures for the poor. If the Company transferred tax-payers' money from the pockets of an Indian nobleman to its own pockets, the transfer might have bankrupted pearl merchants and reduced the number of people in the harem, but would make little difference to the ordinary Indian. The corrupt fiscal practices lasted too short a time, and involved too little money, to sustain a story of permanent impoverishment. The ordinary Indians were quite poor already. There was little that the Company officers could take from them had they tried.

The drain theory, however, did not confine itself only to the 1770s. In the longer run, the Company government initiated a pattern of economic change in India that involved large and sustained payment for services purchased from abroad. The economy maintained a surplus on the trade account, and a deficit on the services account of the balance of payments. The pattern began in the early 1800s or even before (K.N. Chaudhuri's work remains the best study on the early history of the balance of payments), and was sustained right through the colonial period up to the early 1930s. This long-running deficit on the service account was also called a drain by the Indian nationalist writers. The implied thesis was that it was a politically engineered payment, more like a tribute, symbolizing India's abject dependence. Indian economists of an earlier generation debated how large the drain was, and how badly it damaged Indian development.

In the 1970s, Marxist historians offered a reading of the nineteenth-century world economy, in which the empires existed to transfer savings from the poorer regions to the richer ones. The Company's state and the drain of money from India were their favourite examples of exploitation and underdevelopment on a world scale. This reading is too simplistic and has largely been discarded. It is true that the empires did sometimes sponsor organized loot of resources, that they did not necessarily work for the welfare of their subjects, and that the world did become more unequal in the nineteenth century. And yet, transfer of savings cannot be established as the mechanism and the cause of inequality. The empires enabled a diverse range of transactions. All transactions involve payments and receipts. It is impossible to separate the legitimate payments from the tributary or exploitative transactions. The Marxist historians did not supply a convincing way to separate the two types of transactions.

Consequently, most measures of drain remain highly indirect ones, and treat the entire surplus of Indian commodity exports over commodity imports as looted money. This is a mistaken reading of the balance of payments. One would have to be a really naïve economist to treat any income repatriated by foreigners as drain. To use the whole export surplus as a wasteful expenditure misreads Indian history in a fundamental respect. To see how, we need to consider the potential contribution that these payments could make to the economy.

The real puzzle about nineteenth-century India was not that it was a poor country. With the productivity of agricultural land reduced to abysmally low levels by geographic and climatic factors, a rapid economic growth and increasing prosperity without new agricultural technology would have been nothing short of a miracle. No past regime had the necessary knowledge or the resources to bring it about. The real puzzle about India was rather that within the tropical world, which faced quite similar obstacles to economic development, India forged ahead by some key definitions of economic modernization. Compared with colonized Africa and large parts of Asia, India industrialized. In the nineteenth century, employment in factories increased from near zero to more than a million. Cotton textile mills dotted the landscape of Bombay, the mills having been started by merchants and bankers who had been major beneficiaries of Indo-European enterprise. In the same century, India developed one of the biggest railways and telegraphic systems, and had some of the best banks, ports, universities and hospitals in the contemporary world.

By the developing world standards, this efflorescence was exceptional. India at 1800 had goods to sell abroad, but lacked the capital, the skills and the knowledge needed for the establishment of factories, banks, railways and universities. This development was made possible because the scarce inputs were purchased from Britain. The cotton traders of Bombay, for example, sold cotton in Manchester, and procured from Manchester the machinery and the foremen to process cotton in India. In the long run, Indian industrialists reduced the dependence, thanks to the growth of technical and university education within India. The teaching staff in these institutions again was hired from Britain, and their salaries were paid in sterling. In this fashion, nineteenth-century Indian economic growth was reliant on the purchase of services from abroad with money earned by selling goods abroad. A part of these services was tied to the imperial administration and defence. But the major part was payment for services rendered to foreign trade, modern business, education and health.

Dismissing these purchases as a form of tribute might be a patriotic act, but it would be a wrong reading of history. Should we call the salary of the Nobel laureate, Ronald Ross, an employee of the Indian Medical Service, a drain? Should the repatriated profits of tea and jute industries, which provided livelihoods to more than a million Indian peasants, workers and merchants, be described as wasted money? Interest on public debt was another often cited example of drain. All regimes in this time raised loans to finance railway construction and warfare. The true cost of debt depended on which market the loan was raised from, and by this benchmark, London loans were particularly economical. In a broader and long-term perspective, the payment that British India made to Britain for the services of doctors, engineers and professors was a price for skill-building. The return of that process of skill-building is being reaped today in the form of the net income that India receives by selling highly skilled services to the world. It is hard to explain the second kind of flow without the first, colonial, kind.

Much of this development was a later affair. The East India Company started the trajectory, but had neither envisioned nor actively planned for the development of India. Until the 1830s, the Indian administration did not have a serious conception of how to develop India. The Company nevertheless initiated a pattern; it created some of the enabling conditions for an industrialization to unfold in the second half of the nineteenth century. The fact that 80 per cent of factory employment in 1900 was located in or near Bombay, Calcutta and Madras was evidence enough of the enduring legacy of the Company in creating a truly cosmopolitan business culture in India.

All this should not mean that the Company provided the best kind of rule by the eighteenth-century standards.

Conceivably, as a government it could do more than it actually did. Moreover, as Adam Smith and Edmund Burke rightly argued, officers of the state would be unfit to govern if they were allowed to conduct trade on the side. The truth of that proposition was evident enough in the 1770s. To many contemporaries in Britain, the Company rule represented an oppressive regime for its Indian subjects because of the confusion between private interests and public interests.

Indians today know well from the experience of their own world of politics that such confusion can sustain corruption on a large scale; even if the mix is not always injurious to private enterprise.

TIMELINE

1600	East India Company receives charter.
1601–03	James Lancaster leads the first voyage.
1604–06	Second voyage takes place.
1605	Accession of Jahangir.
1607	Third voyage under David Middleton and others. William Hawkins reaches Agra with a letter from James I.
1608	Fourth voyage.
1608–10	Factories established in Surat, Pulicat and Masulipatnam.
1609	Fifth voyage.
1609	Renewal of charter by James I, charter valid in perpetuity.
1610	Sixth voyage under Henry Middleton.
1611–12	The seventh, eighth and the ninth voyages take place.
1612	Thomas Best defeats the Portuguese off Surat (Battle of Swally).
1612	The system of separate voyages ends. Joint-stock voyages begin the next year.
1614–15	Nicholas Downton of the first joint-stock voyage defeats the Portuguese fleet off Surat.

1615–18	Thomas Roe leads mission to India.
1619	First Anglo-Dutch peace treaty.
1622	Company forces defeat the Portuguese in Hormuz.
1623	The 'massacre' of Amboyna.
1627	Accession of Shah Jahan.
1630	Anglo-Portuguese peace treaty of Madrid.
1630	Surat declared the headquarters of the Company's Indian Ocean interests.
1632	Hooghly, a Portuguese settlement, sacked by Shah Jahan.
1633	A party under Ralph Cartwright receives permission to set up a factory in Balasore.
1639	Francis Day builds Fort St George in Madras.
1642	The chief establishment on the east coast officially shifted from Masulipatnam to Madras.
1650	First Company settlement starts in Hooghly.
1653	Madras becomes a 'presidency'.
1654	Second Anglo-Dutch peace treaty.
1657	Renewal of charter by Oliver Cromwell; the joint-stock principle sanctioned.
1659	Accession of Aurangzeb.
1661	Bombay ceded by the Portuguese to the English.
1664	Tea imported by the Company.
1664	Shivaji attacks Surat.
1665	Holland and England at war.
1669	Bombay becomes a property of the Company.
1674	François Martin establishes Pondicherry.
1678	Holland and England restore peace treaty.
1685	The chief establishment on the western coast shifted from Surat to Bombay.

1686	Renewal of charter.
1687	Aurangzeb's Deccan campaign begins; Golkonda falls to the Empire; trade from Masulipatnam suffers.
1687	Chief establishment in Bengal shifts from Hooghly to Calcutta.
1687	Battle between Aurangzeb and the Company.
1688	The Glorious Revolution.
1692	The Commons petitions the king to revoke the charter of the Old Company.
1693	Renewal of charter.
1698	The New East India Company forms.
1700	Parliamentary regulation prohibiting Indian silks.
1707	Aurangzeb dies.
1707	The Company lends money to the British government.
1708	Formation of the United Company of Merchants Trading to the East Indies.
1715	Factory at Canton.
1716	The Company receives, from the Mughal emperor Farrukhsiyar, license to trade for a fixed fee.
1726–28	Mayor's courts started in Bombay, Madras and Calcutta.
1740–48	War of the Austrian Succession.
1746–48	First Carnatic War, the Company loses possession of Madras, moves to Fort St David.
1741	Dupleix appointed governor of Pondicherry.
1744	Robert Clive arrives in Madras.
1748	Treaty of Aix-la-Chapelle ends the War of the Austrian Succession. Madras is restored to the British.

1749–54	Second Carnatic War.
1756–63	Third Carnatic War, Seven Years' War in Europe.
1756	Accession of Siraj-ud-Daula in Bengal.
1756	Clive takes charge as governor of Fort St David.
1757	Battle of Plassey or Palashi (13 June).
1764	Battle of Buxar.
1766	The Company receives 'dewanny' rights of Bengal, Bihar and Orissa.
1765–69	Clive holds office as governor of Bengal.
1766–69	First Anglo-Mysore War; fought on behalf of a combined Maratha-Hyderabad force and lost.
1770	Great Bengal Famine.
1772–73	Warren Hastings is governor of Bengal.
1773	Regulating Act of Lord North. The offices of governor general and Council, and a Supreme Court, created.
1773	Tea Act, intended to establish the Company's monopoly to tea trade in the British empire leads to the Boston Tea Party.
1773	Opium trade declared a government monopoly.
1774–84	Hastings holds office as the first governor general.
1775–82	First Anglo-Maratha War; fought over the Peshwa succession dispute between Raghunathrao (whom the Company helped) and his rivals.
1776	*Wealth of Nations* published.
1780–84	Second Anglo-Mysore War—an extension of the Anglo-French rivalry during the American Revolution—ends with the Peace of Versailles; honours shared.

1781	Select Committee established to report to the Parliament on Indian administration.
1786	William Pitt's East India Company Act formally secures the Parliament's authority to regulate all civil, military and revenue affairs of the Company's territories in India.
1793	Renewal of charter.
1789–92	Third Anglo-Mysore War fought on behalf of Travancore against Tipu Sultan. Tipu loses and cedes large territory.
1799	Tipu Sultan dies in the Fourth Anglo-Mysore War.
1803–05	Second Anglo-Maratha War fought on behalf of Raghunathrao's son Bajirao II with Sindhia, Bhonsla and Holkar forces.
1805	Establishment of Haileybury College to train civilians bound for India.
1813	Promulgation of the Charter Act, leading to the end of the monopoly trading rights in India.
1817–19	Third Anglo-Maratha War, fought with a combined Maratha force.
1833	The Company's commercial powers abolished.
1833	Banking panic in Calcutta following a recession in the indigo trade.
1846	A second panic in Calcutta.
1857	The Indian mutiny.
1858	Government of India Act, 1858; direct British rule of India begins.
1874	The East India Company formally dissolved.

BIBLIOGRAPHY

Early writings: 1650–1950

Anon., *Reflections on the Present State of Our East India Affairs*. London, 1764.

Anon., *British Relations with the Chinese Empire in 1832*. London, 1832.

Begbie, J. *History of the Services of the Madras Artillery with a Sketch of the Rise of the Power of the East India Company in Southern India*, vols. 1–2. Madras, 1852.

Bolts, William. *Considerations on India Affairs; Particularly Respecting the Present State of Bengal and Its Dependencies*. London, 1772.

Bond, E.A., ed. *Speeches of the Managers and Counsel in the Trial of Warren Hastings*, vols. 1–3. London, 1859.

Bowrey, Thomas. *A Geographical Account of Countries Round the Bay of Bengal, 1669 to 1679*. London, 1904.

Braid, William David. *Statement of the East India Company's Conduct towards the Carnatic Stipendiaries*. London, 1853.

Bruce, John. *Annals of the Honorable East India Company from Their Establishment by the Charter of Queen Elizabeth, 1600,* to the Union of the London and English East-India Companies, 1707–08, vols. 1–2. London, 1810.

Carey, W.H. *The Good Old Days of the John Company*. Calcutta, 1882.

Cambridge, Richard Owen. *An Account of the War in India between the English and French on the Coast of Coromandel from the Year 1750 to the Year 1760*. London, 1761.

Dalton, Cornelius. *The Life of Thomas Pitt*. Cambridge, 1915.

Dodwell, H., ed. *The Diary of Ananda Ranga Pillai*, vols. 1–8. Madras, 1922.

F.R. *A Short History of the East India Company*. London, 1793.

Foster, William, ed. *The Journal of John Jourdain, 1608–1617, Describing His Experiences in Arabia, India, and the Malay Archipelago*. Cambridge, 1905.

Fryer, John. *A New Account of East-India and Persia, in Eight Letters*. London, 1698.

Hallward, N.L. *William Bolts: A Dutch Adventurer under John Company*. Cambridge, 1920.

Hill, S.C. *Three Frenchmen in Bengal*. London, 1903.

Hyde, H.B. 'Notes on the Mausoleum of Job Charnock and the Bones Recently Discovered within It', *Proceedings of the Asiatic Society of Bengal*. 1893.

Kaye, John William. *The Administration of the East India Company; a History of Indian Progress*, second edition. London, 1853.

Lockyer, Charles. *An Account of the Trade in India*. London, 1711.

Macaulay, Thomas Babington. *The History of England from the Accession of James the Second*, vols. 1–10. London.

Macpherson, James. *The History and Management of the East-India Company from Its Origin in 1600 to the Present Times*, vols. 1–2. London, 1782.

Malleson, G.B. *History of the French in India*. London, 1893.

Markham, Clements. *The Voyages of Sir James Lancaster, Kt., to the East Indies*. London, 1877.

Masulipatnam Consultation Book of 1682–83. Madras, 1916.

Mill, John Stuart. *Memorandum of the Improvements in the Administration of India During the last Thirty Years and the Petition of the East-India Company to Parliament*. London, 1858.

Mittra, Bipin Bihari. *Maharaja Nabakrishna Deb Bahadur* (in Bengali). Calcutta, 1879.

Morse, H.B. *The Chronicles of the East India Company Trading to China, 1635–1834*, vols. 1–4. Oxford, 1926.

Mukhopadhyay, H. *Kalikata: Sekaler o Ekaler* (in Bengali). Calcutta, 1915.

Neill, J.G.S. *Historical Record of the Honorable East India Company's First Madras European Regiment*. London, 1843.

Owen, Sidney. *The Seige of Madras*. Woolwich, 1867.

———. *Dupleix and the Empire of India*. New York, 1887.

Orme, Robert. *Historical Fragments of the Mogul Empire, of the Morattoes, and of the English Concerns in Indostan from the year MDCLIX*. London, 1805.

Pennant, Thomas. *The View of Hindoostan*, vols. 1–2. London, 1798.

Robinson, F.P. *The Trade of the East India Company from 1709 to 1813*. Cambridge, 1912.

Rundall, Thomas. *Narratives of Voyages towards the North-West in Search of a Passage to Cathay and India, 1496 to 1631*. London, 1849.

Ryley, J. Horton. *Ralph Fitch*. London, 1899.

Scott, William. *The Constitution and Finance of English, Scottish and Irish Joint-Stock Companies to 1720,* vol. 2. Cambridge, 1910.

Smith, Adam. *An Inquiry into the Nature and Causes of the Wealth of Nations*. New York, 1994.

Stanhope, Philip. *Genuine Memoirs of Asiaticus*. London, 1784.

Stavorinus, John Splinter. *Voyage to the East Indies*. London, 1798.

Symson, William. *A New Voyage to the East Indies*. London, 1715.

Temple, Richard, ed. *The Diaries of Streynsham Master 1675–1680*, vols. 1–2. London, 1911.

Verelst, Harry. *A View of the Rise, Progress, and Present State of the English Government in Bengal*. London, 1772.

Wheeler, J. Talboys. *Early Records of British India*. Calcutta, 1879.

Willson, Beckles. *Ledger and Sword: Or the Honourable Company of Merchants of England Trading to the East Indies (1599–1874)*, vols 1–2. London, 1903.

Wilson, C.R. *Early Annals of the English in Bengal*, vols. 1–2. London, 1895.

Wright, Arnold. *Early English Adventurers in the East*. New York, 1917.

——. *Annesley of Surat and His Times, the True Story of the Mythical Wesley Fortune*. London, 1918.

Recent scholarship: 1950–2011

Adams, Julia. 'Trading States, Trading Places: The Role of Patrimonialism in Early Modern Dutch Development'. *Comparative Studies in Society and History*. 1994.

Bayly, C.A. *Rulers, Townsmen and Bazaars: North Indian Society in the Age of British Expansion 1770–1870*. Cambridge. 1983.

Blitz, Rudolph C. 'Mercantilist Policies and the Pattern of World Trade, 1500–1750'. *Journal of Economic History (JEH)*. 1967.

Bohun, James. 'Protecting Prerogative: William III and the East India Trade Debate, 1689–1698'. *Past Imperfect*. 1993.

Bowen, H.V. 'Investment and Empire in the Later Eighteenth Century: East India Stockholding, 1756–1791'. *Economic History Review (EHR)*. 1989.

——. 'The Little Parliament: The General Court of the East India Company, 1750–1784'. *The Historical Journal*. 1991.

——. 'Sinews of Trade and Empire: The Supply of Commodity Exports to the East India Company during the Late Eighteenth Century'. *EHR*. 2002.

——. 'Bullion for Trade, War, and Debt-Relief: British Movements of Silver to, around, and from Asia, 1760–1833', *Modern Asian Studies (MAS)*. 2010.

——. *The Business of Empire: The East India Company and Imperial Britain, 1756–1833*. Cambridge, 2006.

Bowyer, T.H. 'India and the Personal Finances of Philip Francis'. *EHR*. 1995.

Brenner, Robert. 'The Social Basis of English Commercial Expansion, 1550-1650'. *JEH*. 1972.

Brennig, Joseph J. 'Chief Merchants and the European Enclaves of Seventeenth Century Coromandel'. *MAS*. 1977.

Cain, P.J., and Hopkins, A.G. 'Gentlemanly Capitalism and British Expansion Overseas: The Old Colonial System, 1688–1850'. *HER*. 1986.

Carlos, Ann M., and Nicholas, Stephen. 'Giants of an Earlier Capitalism: The Chartered Trading Companies as Modern Multinationals'. *Business History Review*. 1988.

——. 'Theory and History: Seventeenth-Century Joint-Stock Chartered Trading Companies'. *JEH*. 1996.

Chaudhuri, K.N. 'The East India Company and the Export of Treasure in the Early Seventeenth Century'. *EHR*. 1963.

——. 'India's Foreign Trade and the Cessation of the East India Company's Trading Activities, 1828–40'. *EHR*. 1966.

——. 'Treasure and Trade Balances: The East India Company's Export Trade, 1660–1720'. *EHR*. 1968.

——. *The Trading World of Asia and the English East India Company, 1660–1760*. Cambridge. 1978.

Chaudhury, Sushil. *From Prosperity to Decline: Eighteenth-Century Bengal*. Delhi, 1995.

Dasgupta, Ashin. *The World of the Indian Ocean Merchant, 1500–1800*. Delhi, 2001.

Datta, Kalikinkar. *Shah Alam II and the East India Company*. Calcutta, 1965.

Datta, K.K. 'India's Trade with Europe and America in the Eighteenth Century', *Journal of the Economic and Social History of the Orient (JESHO)*. 1959.

Davis, Ralph. 'English Foreign Trade, 1660–1700'. *EHR*. 1954.

Desai, Ashok. 'The Origins of Parsi Enterprise', *Indian Economic and Social History Review*. 1968.

Ekelund, Jr, Robert B., and Tollison, Robert D. 'Mercantilist Origins of the Corporation', *Bell Journal of Economics*, 11(2). 1980.

Ferrier, R.W. 'The Armenians and the East India Company in Persia in the Seventeenth and Early Eighteenth Centuries'. *HER*. 1973.

Flynn, Dennis, and Girladez, Arturo, 'Cycles of Silver: Global

Economic Unity through the Mid-Eighteenth Century'. *Journal of World History*. 2002.

Foster, William, 'Charles I and the East India Company', *EHR*. 1904.

Freedman, Paul. *Out of the East: Spices and the Medieval Imagination*. New Haven. 2008.

Furber, Holden. *John Company at Work: A Study of European Expansion in India in the Late Eighteenth Century*. Cambridge. 1951.

Ghosh, Durba. *Sex and the Family in Colonial India*. Cambridge. 2006.

Gupta, Bishnupriya. 'Competition and Control in the Market for Textiles: Indian Weavers and the English East India Company in the Eighteenth Century'. In Giorgio Riello and Tirthankar Roy, eds. *How India Clothed the World: The World of South Asian Textiles, 1500–1850*. Leiden, 2009.

Gupta, Brijen K. *Sirajuddaullah and the East India Company, 1756–1757*. Leiden, 1962.

Harris, Abram L. 'John Stuart Mill: Servant of the East India Company'. *Canadian Journal of Economics and Political Science*. 1964.

Hasan, Farhat. 'Indigenous Cooperation and the Birth of a Colonial City: Calcutta, c. 1698–1750', *MAS*, 1992.

Hejeebu, Santhi. 'Contract Enforcement in the English East India Company'. *JEH*. 2005.

Horwitz, Henry. 'The East India Trade, the Politicians, and the Constitution: 1689–1702'. *Journal of British Studies*. 1978.

Hossain, Hameeda. *The Company Weavers of Bengal: The East India Company and the Organisation of Textile Production in Bengal 1750-1813*. Delhi. 1989.

Joslin, D.M. 'London Private Bankers, 1720–1785'. *EHR*. 1954.

Karim, A. 'Murshid Kuli Khan's Relations with the English East India Company from 1700–1707'. *JESHO*. 1961.

Khan, Shafaat Ahmed. *Anglo Portuguese Negotiations Relating to Bombay 1660–1677*. Allahabad. 1922.

Kranton R., and Swamy, A. 'Contracts, Hold-up, and Exports: Textiles and Opium in Colonial India'. *American Economic Review*. 2008.

Lewis, Archibald. 'Maritime Skills in the Indian Ocean 1368–1500'. *JESHO*. 1973.

Mallick, Binoy S. 'English Trade and Indigenous Finance in Bengal and Gujarat in the Seventeenth Century: A Study of Dadni System and the Rate of Interest'. *Studies in History*. 1986.

Marshall, P.J. 'British Society in India under the East India Company'. *MAS*. 1997.

——. *The Making and Unmaking of Empires: Britain, India, and America, c. 1750–1783*. Oxford. 2005.

Mukherjee, Mithi. 'Justice, War, and the Imperium: India and Britain in Edmund Burke's Prosecutorial Speeches in the Impeachment Trial of Warren Hastings'. *Law and History Review*. 2005.

Mukund, Kanakalatha. *The View from Below: Indigenous Society, Temples and the Early Colonial State in Tamil Nadu. 1700–1835*. Hyderabad. 2005.

Neal, Larry. 'Integration of International Capital Markets: Quantitative Evidence from the Eighteenth to Twentieth Centuries'. *JEH*. 1985.

Nightingale, Pamela. *Trade and Empire in Western India, 1784–1806*. Cambridge. 1970.

The Oxford Dictionary of National Biography, various entries.

Parthasarathi, Prasannan. *The Transition to a Colonial Economy, Weavers, Merchants and Kings in South India, 1720–1800*. Cambridge. 2001.

Philips, C.H. 'The Secret Committee of the East India Company, 1784–1858'. *Bulletin of the School of Oriental and African Studies*. 1940.

——. 'The East India Company "Interest" and the English Government, 1783–84'. *Transactions of the Royal Historical Society*. 1937.

Platt, Virginia. 'The East India Company and the Madagascar Slave Trade'. *The William and Mary Quarterly*. 1969.

Plummer, Alfred. *The London Weavers' Company 1600–1970*. London. 1972.

Prakash, Om. *European Commercial Enterprise in Pre-Colonial India*. Cambridge. 1998.

——. 'The Indian Maritime Merchant, 1500–1800'. *JESHO*. 2004.

Quennell, Peter, ed. *The Memoirs of William Hickey*. London. 1960.

Roy, Tirthankar. *Company of Kinsmen: Enterprise and Community in South Asian History*. Delhi. 2010.

——. *The Economic History of India 1757–2010*. Delhi. 2011.

Schmitthoff, M. 'The Origin of the Joint-Stock Company'. *The University of Toronto Law Journal*, 3(1). 1939.

Sen, Sudipta. *Empire of Free Trade: The East India Company and the Making of the Colonial Marketplace*. Philadelphia. 1998.

Serajuddin, A.M. 'The Salt Monopoly of the East India Company's Government in Bengal'. *JESHO*. 1978.

Siddiqi, Asiya. 'Money and Prices in the Earlier Stages of Empire: India and Britain 1760–1840'. *Indian Economic Social History Review*. 1981.

Sinha, J.C. 'Economic Theorists among the Servants of John Company (1766–1806)'. *Economic Journal*. 1925.

Spear, Percival. *The Nabobs*. Richmond. 1980.

Srinivasachari, C.S. *History of the City of Madras Written for the Tercentenary Celebration Committee, 1939*. Madras. 1939.

Steensgaard, Niels. *The Asian Trade Revolution of the Seventeenth Century*. Chicago. 1974.

Stern, Philip J. *The Company-State: Corporate Sovereignty and the Early Modern Foundations of the British Empire in India*. New York. 2011.

Subrahmanyam, Sanjay. 'Rural Industry and Commercial Agriculture in Late Seventeenth Century South-Eastern India'. *Past and Present*. 1990.

———. 'Of Imarat and Tijarat: Asian Merchants and State Power in the Western Indian Ocean, 1400 to 1750'. *Comparative Studies in Society and History*. 1995.

Subramanian, Lakshmi. *Indigenous Capital and Imperial Expansion: Bombay, Surat and the West Coast*. Delhi. 1996.

Sutherland, L.S. 'The East India Company in Eighteenth-Century Politics'. *EHR*. 1947.

———. 'The East India Company and the Peace of Paris'. *HER*. 1947.

Swai, Bonaventure. 'East India Company and Moplah Merchants of Tellicherry: 1694–1800'. *Social Scientist*. 1979.

Swarnalatha, P. 'Revolt, Testimony, Petition: Artisanal Protests in Colonial Andhra', *International Review of Social History*. 2001.

Torri, Michelguglielmo. 'Mughal Nobles, Indian Merchants and the Beginning of British Conquest in Western India: The Case of Surat 1756–1759'. *MAS*. 1998.

Waddell, David. 'Charles Davenant and the East India Company'. *Economica*. 1956.

Ward, J.R. 'The Industrial Revolution and British Imperialism, 1750–1850'. *EHR*. 1994.

Washbrook, David. 'South India 1770–1840: The Colonial Transition'. *MAS*. 2004.

Webster, Anthony. 'The Political Economy of Trade Liberalization: The East India Company Charter Act of 1813'. *EHR*. 1990.

——. *The Twilight of the East India Company: The Evolution of Anglo-Asian Commerce and Politics, 1790–1860*. Woodbridge. 2009.